TENNYSON'S "EPIC DRAMA"

ELTON EDWARD SMITH

University Press of America, Inc.
Lanham • New York • Oxford

Copyright © 1997 by
University Press of America,® Inc.
4720 Boston Way
Lanham, Maryland 20706

12 Hid's Copse Rd.
Cummor Hill, Oxford OX2 9JJ

Library of Congress Cataloging-in-Publication Data

Smith, Elton Edward
Tennyson's "epic drama" / Elton Edward Smith.
p. cm.
Includes bibliographical references and index.
1. Tennyson, Alfred Tennyson, Baron, 1809-1892--Dramatic works.
2. Verse drama, English--History and criticism. I. Title.
PR5592.D7S65   1997   822'.8--dc21   97-29659 CIP

ISBN 0-7618-0875-2 (cloth: alk. ppr.)

⊖™ The paper used in this publication meets the minimum
requirements of American National Standard for information
Sciences—Permanence of Paper for Printed Library Materials,
ANSI Z39.48—1984

Contents

Acknowledgments

Since a number of years elapsed between my *The Two Voices: a Tennyson Study* and this, its sequel, *Tennyson's "Epic Drama,"* I wish to express my deepest appreciation to all who have encouraged me along the way, especially:

The Lord Noël Annan
Kevin Taylor, Cambridge University
Holly Panich, Ohio University
Thomas Collins, University of Western Ontario
Amanda Irwin, Scarecrow Press
Nancy Ulrich, University Press of America
Prof. Gary Olson and the University of South Florida
    Publications Council

This volume was published in part through the gracious assistance of the University of South Florida Publications Council.

Introduction

Although Lord Tennyson has always been a staple of Victorian criticism, there seems to be a current revival of interest: Linda Hughes, *The Many Facèd Glass*, Ohio University 1987; Elaine Jordan, *Alfred Tennyson*, Cambridge University 1988; Kenneth McKay, *Many Glancing Colours*, University of Toronto 1988; Roger Platizby, *A Blueprint of His Dissent*, Bucknell University 1989; Gerhard Joseph, *Tennyson and the Text*, Cambridge University 1992; Philip Collins, ed., *Tennyson: Seven Essays*, St. Martin's 1992; Michael Thorn, *Tennyson*, St. Martin's 1993; Peter Levi, *Tennyson*, Scribner's 1994

A commonplace of literary criticism has been the pejorative judgment on 19th century drama—with the exceptions of the drawing-room comedies of Oscar Wilde and the early problem plays of George Bernard Shaw. Yet Alfred, Lord Tennyson devoted valuable years and all his rich gifts on plays that he considered to be the best work he had done, and, like the *Idylls of the King*, to form an epical history of England.

This trilogy of plays pourtrays the making of England. In *Harold* we have the great conflict between Danes, Saxons, and Normans for supremacy, the awakening of the English people and clergy from the slumber into which they had for the most part fallen, and the forecast of the greatness of our composite race. In *Becket* the struggle is between the Crown and the Church for predominance, a struggle which continued for many centuries. In *Mary* are described the final downfall of Roman Catholicism in England, and the dawning of a new age; for after the era of priestly domination comes the era of the freedom of the individual.

"In *The Foresters*," my father wrote, "I have sketched the state of the people in another great transition period of the making of England, when the barons sided with the people and eventually won for them the Magna Carta."

(*Memoir*, volume ii, page 173)

Since, when they are read at all, they reveal the same poetic genius that Tennyson displayed in dramatic monologue, elegy, and epic, I wonder if it is not time to re-evaluate and perhaps even to rehabilitate his large and rich dramatic production, including such juvenilia as *The Devil and the Lady*, such mature plays as *Queen Mary* 1875, *Harold* 1876, *The Falcon* 1879, *The Promise of May* 1882, *The Cup* 1884, *Becket* 1884; *Maud*, which he himself called a "monodrama," and with possible consideration of *The Idylls of the King* and *The Princess* as essentially dramatic oeuvres?

When the dramas receive critical attention at all, it is usually to: a. arbitrarily dismiss, as in Christopher Rick's otherwise admirable anthology (omitted "only in part on a judgement of their quality"), or b. pejoratively relate Tennyson drama to the florid acting styles and melodramatic plots that dominated the Victorian stage, cf. Robert Bernard Martin's denunciation of spectacular productions, oversized theaters requiring "ringing set speeches, heroic [or, at least broad] acting, voices and gestures" (*The Unquiet Heart*, 1980).

On the other hand, an academic friend, Provost Thomas J. Collins, The University of Western Ontario, informed me that Garland Press is publishing his Tennyson Concordance keyed to Ricks' Longman's text 1987, which excluded the plays. Thus as a necessary companion piece, they would publish an annotated edition (with introduction, variants etc.) of Tennyson's plays.

Tennyson would not have lightly dismissed his plays from critical consideration. Writing about the last Saxon king (Harold), the first Plantagenet king (Henry II, *Becket*), and the last Catholic Queen (*Mary*) he had deliberately courted the comparison with Shakespeare's historical drama, as the Victorian age liked to think of itself as "a new Elizabethan age" (Martin). As Linda Hughes points out (*The Many Facèd Glass*), he must have considered them to be of value because he wrote his first extraordinary unfinished drama when he was only fourteen in his father's rectory, but then, at sixty-five, went ahead to write seven more plays within an eight-year period! Peter Thomason reminds us that five of his plays were "performed during his life, and he died exactly four months before the brilliant opening night of a sixth." Only one can be said certainly to have failed in production. This is a theatrical record, second to no nineteenth-century poet's (*Tennyson*, D.J. Palmer, ed. 1973).

A late contemporary of Tennyson, J. Cuming Walters, could write in 1893 about *The Falcon*: "its triviality of treatment and its staleness of subject would render it unmeet for serious criticism, even if it were redeemed by a single passage worthy of remembrance;" but then would add the caveat that the first five plays "contain some of Tennyson's best thoughts and prepare for the late dramas (*The Cup* and *The Promise of May*) in which he came near achieving absolute success" (*Tennyson, Poet, Philosopher, Idealist*). It is also notable that he found *The Foresters* (universally neglected), "the last and best of its class, the one of the least ambitious, it is almost a flawless piece of workmanship—an idyll glowing with colour, a poem sparkling and spontaneous, a drama skillful and impressive."

Other more major contemporaries expressed varied admiration. Sir Richard Jebb (editor of Sophocles) claimed *Becket* to be "a drama of great power, finely conceived and finely executed" and compared its theme to the religion/state tension of *Antigone*. The *Times* and the *Spectator* placed *Queen Mary*, Tennyson's favorite, high above the "ordinary work of Shakespeare, and only little lower than his highest." J.A. Froude considered *Queen Mary* the "greatest of your works." and chuckled, "you have hit Manning and Company a more fatal blow than a thousand pamphleteers and controversialists." Henry Irving claimed that *Becket* provided him with one of his three greatest stage triumphs.

The Prime Minister, W.E. Gladstone was "glad that, in turning to historic times, you have struck a stroke for the nation." Robert Browning, who considered *Queen Mary* to be "astonishingly fine," lauded the production aspects in a letter to Tennyson, April 19, 1876:

> I want to be among the earliest who assure you of the complete success of your "Queen Mary" last night. I have more than once seen a more satisfactory performance of it, to be sure, in what Carlyle calls "the Private Theatre under my own hat," because there and then not a line nor a word was left out; nay, there were abundant "encores" of half the speeches: still whatever was left by the stage scissors suggested what a quantity of "cuttings" would furnish one with an afterfeast.

Introduction

At the performance to which Browning referred, "one of the lines most heartily applauded was: 'I am English Queen, not Roman Emperor'— which hit the temper of the London democracy, for the Queen had lately assumed the title of Empress of India" (*Memoir*, ii, 185).

The organizational strategy I am projecting focuses first on what Tennyson himself thought about *The Devil and the Lady*, written 1823-1824; *Queen Mary*, published 1875; *Harold*, published 1876; *Becket*, 1876-1879; *The Falcon*, produced 1879; *The Cup*, produced 1881; *The Promise of May*, produced 1882; *The Foresters*, produced 1892. This division will depend heavily upon *Alfred Lord Tennyson: A Memoir by His Son*; Charles Tennyson, *Alfred Tennyson*; *The Letters of Alfred, Lord Tennyson*, Cecil Lang and Edgar Shannon Jr., editors.

The next major division of the study would consist of a critical analysis of each of the eight plays, always embedding them within the context of his major works and especially of the later works being written contemporaneously with the writing of the dramas. For example *The Promise of May* would be related to another domestic idyll, "Enoch Arden;" a contrast would be drawn among the queens of the drama, *Queen Mary*, the toast, "To the Queen!" and *The Idylls of the King*. The third major division of the study would provide a consideration of the plays in terms of dramaturgy, i.e., plot, character, setting, theme and effectiveness on the stage. This effectiveness would be tested by the melodramatic milieu of the Victorian Age as well as by the dominant melodramatic structure of our own contemporary drama: violence, sexuality, the chase, the hairbreadth escape, villains, heroes, and the final victory of virtue. Perhaps the famous Tennyson melancholia will prove more attractive to a postmodern audience than it was to the ebullient Victorians.

In *Two Voices: A Tennyson Study*, I objected vigorously to Sir Harold Nicolson's attempt to partition the laureate's productivity (*Tennyson, Aspect of His Life, Character and Poetry*). Dividing his works into four overlapping periods: 1. 1827-1842 "imitative Keatsian;" 2. 1835-1855 "most important lyrical period;" 3. 1857-1879 "the most unfortunate, mid-Victorian period;" 4. 1880-1892 "the splendid Aldworth period;" he hoped to produce a revival of interest in Tennyson's poetry by discarding large parts of it!

The critical battle against partition has been largely won—it is unlikely that a modern critic will pick two periods of his work to praise and two to blame. But the generic partition continues: Anything of Tennyson except the Idylls; Anything except the dialect poems; or Everything except the plays.

It remains my contention that the measure of Tennyson can be taken only by the consideration of all his work. This study would attempt to embed his plays within his other major works as revealing evidences of who Tennyson was and the nature of his poetical genius expressed in all his genres.

Chapter I

౭ට൚

A Fourteen-Year-Old Playwright:
The Devil and the Lady 1823

"I [Hallam, Lord Tennyson] have published 'The Devil and the Lady' because of the note in my grandfather, Dr. Tennyson's handwriting to the effect that the comedy was composed by my father at the early age of fourteen [this note is written on the Trinity manuscript']."

What a striking contrast is provided by the small brown-covered notebook, only 5½ inches by 3 inches, written earlier than the Cambridge manuscript. Side by side lie the scrawling school-boy lettering and the scratchy drawings and then the exquisite handwriting of the text—as if a child had scribbled illustrations on an adult's work. But, as Bernard Groom explained: "There were no profound changes in Tennyson's diction during the course of his long poetic career. . . . Tennyson attained a characteristic style early in his career and he never lost it . . . " (*Society for Pure English*, Bernard Groom, "On the diction of Tennyson, Browning and Arnold, tract No. *LIII* Oxford, 1939; 97-98). The scrawling of the schoolboy and the writing of a precocious teen-age genius.

But the Latin epigraph goes far to reveal the sensitive boy beneath the premature playwright: *Spes Alit juventutem et poesin, vituperatio premit et laudet.* It was hope that nourished his youthful genius against the parental harshness that would diminish and erase it. This from a boy who ten years later would be silenced from poetry for a decade by the fairly mild critical "vituperation" of 1833. But early talent was not without companionship: Charles (the other brother of *Poems by Two Brothers*) April 20, 1827, also wrote a play, unfortunately lost in much the same manner and at the same time.

Charles Tennyson, grandson of Alfred, was positive none of the juvenile drama was written after Alfred's sixteenth birthday, and advanced the unexceptionable critical judgment that while the form and manner were secondhand from Elizabethan and Jacobean playwrights, the style and themes were both original and characteristic. "This play, written when the poet was only fourteen years old, is a brilliant experiment in the vein of the Elizabethan comedy, showing a command of versification, a richness of language and imagery, a vivacity of humor and a range of knowledge which are positively astounding" (Charles Tennyson, ed. *The Devil and the Lady and Unpublished Early Poems* p. *vi*). With greater restraint, the unrelated critic Jerome Hamilton Buckley judiciously admits the remarkable vigor of the style while opining that the play imitated "as much of an Elizabethan gusto of speech as a remarkable boy of fourteen could master" (*The Poems of Tennyson*, *xi*).

The theme of the struggle between husband and wife for dominance is at least as old in world literature as the Old Testament juxtaposition of Jezebel, "woman of splendid evil," alongside King Ahab, who, denied a neighboring vineyard, retreats to his bed to sulk; whereas his queen simply goes out and gets Naboth's vineyard, thus proving a Queen can be more kingly than the King. In British letters, Chaucer's wife of Bath solidly supports the sovereignty of wives over husbands. The exaggerated concern for a wife's honor when her husband is absent is strongly reminiscent of Shakespeare's Moor of Venice or Webster's Duchess of Malfi, in striking contrast with the Restoration assumption that cuckolding a husband is the stuff of comedy, not tragedy.

The most surprising aspect of this fragment of a play is the exuberant gusto of language and the violence of relationship. Charles Tennyson attributes these unlikely qualities to boyish passion: "In its exuberance of language, its crude schoolboy humor, the vivacity of its character drawing, its boyishly passionate aspiration, so urgent that it often finds utterance through the mouth of the Devil himself, it seems to me to stand most firmly on its own base, a living and personal thing" (*xii*). Although he argues that this work of the boy Tennyson should help us solve the "enigma of Tennyson the man," it remains undeniable that this lonely wife's plans for sexual entertainment are very different from the monotonic melancholy of Marianna in her moated grange or the Lady of Shalott in her funeral boat. Instead of lamenting musically "he will not come," Amoret ("Jessica" in the first-draft) rejoices that her eighty-year-old husband's sea voyage will keep him long from home, so the warm-blooded young wife plans erotic badinage to fill every moment of his absence.

The male characters—Magus and his obedient Devil—on the other hand, are subject to all the doubts and uncertainties of "The Coach of Death" 1823 or 1824, "The Vision of Sin" 1842, "Perdidi Diem" (Begun at Somersby, completed at Trinity college), "The Supposed Confessions" 1830, or "The Two Voices" 1833.

His estimate of the power of twenty-year-old female hormones leads even the Devil to complain that "to guard / A woman 'gainst her will" is a difficult assignment, with the tacit expectation that somehow her subtle wit will foil his watchfulness. Against mere males the Devil can boast with boyish triumph; "And having punched him fundamentally / With my strong hooves, I left him bruised and battered / As a beefsteak" (Act I, Scene *ii*). Magus is violent only in his anger; in calmer moments he philosophizes that possession always produces anxiety (Scene *iii*). But his violence cannot hold candle to the rage of the young wife in her furious soliloquy after Magus departs: "Grasshopper, / Consuming the green promise of my youth!" (Scene *iv*). Whereas he thinks of himself merely as the custodian of beauty: "For in life's passage would I always look / Upon that side of things which showeth fairest."

The basis of the *Dramatis Personae* is the "comedy of humors," in which each person suffers the dominance of a single gland by which characters may be classified as choleric, asthenic, athletic or melancholic. Of course this medical theory had been a molding power in Ben Jonson's comedy *Every Man in his Humor*, 1598. Thus the "Induction" to *Every Man Out of His Humor*, 1599 explicates:

> Some one peculiar quality
> Doth so possess a man, that it doth draw
> All his affects, his spirits, and his powers,
> In their confluctions, all to run one way.

The predecessors of this character-writing include the ancient Greek essayist Theophrastus, Bishop Joseph Hall 1608, Francis Bacon, Sir Thomas Overbury 1614. Thus the young lad, other than the complex three-dimensional figures of the Magus, Amoret, and the Devil, is content to show us a lawyer, an apothecary, a sailor, an astronomer, a soldier, and a monk. Although each is given a personal name, all are essentially two-dimensional characters operating out of a single dominant glandular secretion appropriate to their vocations.

The divisions of the drama bow to the Gallic Four Unities and chop everything into the short scenes created by a major entrance or exit.

In blank verse, Magus invokes a servitor Devil, who immediately responds in the German tradition of a clownish oaf, rather than the grand Mephisto Devil of the Italian and British writers. The full apparatus of necromancy includes: invocation by use of demonic names, the drawing of a cabalistic circle, the setting in a forest under a night storm. In vigorous fustian quite unlike his later melancholia, a poet T.S. Eliot described as "the great master of metric as well as melancholia . . . the saddest of all English poets" (*Essays*, p. 175); the young poet clothes his thought in flaunting, boastful language which even the Magus describes as "heroics." To the Devil, who hears Amoret's furious soliloquy and disapproves, woman's tears are despicable weapons and human moralizing irrelevant. This from a poet who will write hundreds of lines about "Tears" and who will most often speak out of the contrarieties of a moral morass!

Appropriately, the first candidate for *amour* is Antonio, and lawyer-like, his seduction is through the witty dialectic of scholasticism. To her ardent rebuke that wind and rain could not deter a true lover, he calmly replies that he prefers to be a "comfortable lover" (Act II. Sc. ii). The Devil, ready to pounce upon this unardent swain, is interrupted by the appearance of Pharmaceuticus, who wishes to apply the diagnoses of Humor to his competitor, Antonio, to see if he be hypochondriacal or hysteric. Antonio tells him to go to the Devil, who is naturally offended. At this point the dialogue descends to the elaborate name-calling and peasant insults of the morality plays, in turn interrupted by the Sailor's arrival, along with Angulo (astronomer), Campano (soldier) and Benedict (monk), permitting the boy playwright to indulge in double puns: not only are the suitors all expressions of the humors, their very names derive from their vocations.

Like Chaucer's Pardoner in the *Canterbury Tales*, the monk Benedict claims to have come only to show Amoret a "piece of the true Cross inclosed/ In chrystal" (Act II, Sc *vii*). Then the Devil, disguised in scholastic cap and gown (assumed by the suitors to be Amoret playing a costume game), like the later Wagnerian Tannhauser, invites all the suitors to enter for a singing contest to express their burning love for their eager hostess, who has already set the table with an abundance of meats and wines.

The third act begins with a flurry of puns and *doubles entendres*, in which Stephanio the sailor calls Benedict "a fine cargo of guts," and the monk, protesting that he never drinks, then drinks profusely in order to stop the execrations of the other suitors for the lady's favors. Antonio, ready to fight, is amazed by the strength of the Devil (assumed to be Amoret), when he lands abruptly on his back. The songs that follow the violent horseplay establish the pattern of the interspersed lyric so useful to the mature Tennyson in *Maud* 1855, "The Lotos-Eaters" 1833, *The Princess* 1847, etc.

A Macbethian "Knocking at the door" sends everyone scurrying for a hiding place. Foiled of sea-passage by a storm, the Magus vows to torment the Devil if he has betrayed his trust and, quite missing the point, chides his demonic minion for his female disguise. In the same scene (Act III, Sc. ii), the fourteen-year-old playwright, himself on the threshold of adolescence, muses on the manhood that lies ahead:

> When couched in Boyhood's passionless tranquility,
> The natural mind of man is warm and yielding,
> Fit to receive the best impressions,
> But raise it to the atmosphere of manhood
> And the rude breath of dissipation
> Will harden it to stone.

One can only conjecture whether this observation was based on the rural manhood of his father's parish or on the alcoholic dissipations of the Reverend George Clayton Tennyson himself.

While the Magus hides to watch and listen, "jealousy personified," the suitors tentatively slink out of hiding. The Devil encourages their self-exposure with the convenient lie that the knocker was only an old, discarded suitor and then maliciously proceeds to describe with sharp accuracy, the ugliness of the hidden Magus who is forced to listen in silence.

Now that they are all exposed to the unexpectedly-returned master of the cottage, the Devil decides it time to unveil, the better to pummel the miscreants, but not before one last pun by Pharmaceuticus who wooes Amoret/Devil as "my flower of sulphur." The Devil muses "that's a *home* touch, though but a random hit" as the manuscript ends abruptly. Charles Tennyson thought that although Alfred Tennyson revised his work so extensively, none of this dramatic fragment was written after the poet was sixteen and that he never had any intention of completing it, considering his own juvenilia to be of dubious value: the epigraph of *Poems of Two Brothers* was Martial's *"Haec nos. norimus esse nihil"*— We ourselves know that these are nothing.

In a much later critical comment, Michael Thorn (*Tennyson*) reminds us of two salient poles of reaction. This is the word of a fourteen-year-old. "Its similes are often based on schoolboy mathematics, with conceits made out of such themes as vulgar fractions and recurring decimals. . . ." Nevertheless, it is also "one of the most impressive pieces of juvenilia left behind by a writer" (pp. 21, 22), The second scene of the third act which contains a meditation on man's folly, his upward struggle despite temptation, and the phantom nature of all his understanding, is staggering in view of the mature poet's exploration of precisely these themes.

> The summer fly
> That skims the surface of the deep black pod
> Knows not the gulf beneath its slippery path.
> Man sees, but plunges madly into it.
> We follow through a night of crime and care
> The voice of soft temptation, still it calls,
> And still we follow onwards, till we find
> She is a Phantom—and we follow still.

Having referred extensively to Tennyson's fragmentary drama of 1823, it is helpful to place that fragment in the mass of work produced so early by a boy who, at the age of five announced: "I hear a voice that's speaking in the wind," and not long afterward placed in his brother's hands a slate covered with blank verse on the subject assigned by Charles (only one year his senior) the flowers in the rectory garden. Having used Thomson's *Seasons* as the only model he knew, the child awaited his sibling's verdict: "Yes, you can write" (Anne Thackeray Ritchie, *Records of Tennyson Ruskin, Browning*, New York 1892). His grandfather, commissioning the child to write an elegy on his grandmother, gave him ten shillings and made the thunderously mistaken prophecy: "There, that is the first money you have earned by your poetry, and take my word for it, it will be the last." This to a poet who became a Lord of the realm, occupied two country estates and a house in London, and in 1850 was appointed Poet Laureate of England by an appreciative Queen!

In 1826, when Alfred was seventeen, the brothers were preparing a volume of 102 poems, published early in 1827 by Messrs. Jackson, booksellers and printers in Louth (where Charles and Alfred were still students in the local grammar school), who paid twenty pounds for the copyright. Like the gifted Brontë children, young Tennysons, after playing at knights and jousting awkwardly but enthusiastically during the long summer weeks at the Somersby Rectory, when they came to Sunday dinner, each deposited a chapter of mock-historical romance beneath the potato bowl. Brother Frederick also wrote poetry, contributing four selections to *Poems by Two Brothers* and later publishing several volumes of poetry.

The story has often been told about the Trinity College gold medal poem "Timbuctoo" 1828. At the time Alfred went up to Cambridge University, he wrote "The Lover's Tale" (not published until several years later), and the following summer at the insistence of his father, who considered that his son was doing little, he took his poem of 1826 "The Battle of Armageddon," provided a new beginning and ending, and submitted it as "Timbuctoo" in the competition for the Chancellor's Prize. To retailor a poem on the last great battle of apocalyptic history into an exotic picture of a mythical kingdom boggles the imagination, but also reminds us that Tennyson saved all his poetic scraps (witness the organization of *In Memoriam A.H.H.*) and habitually recycled them into new situations and settings. Nevertheless the young poet won the Gold Medal, and the universally admired Arthur Hallam, with his *terza rima* in the style of Dante, was unsuccessful.

Starting out like Coleridge's "Kubla Khan" and ending like Byron's "Darkness," "Timbuctoo" includes the Elegy's phrase "shocks of change" and is startlingly similar to the 95th canto of Tennyson's *In Memoriam, A.H.H.* The Coleridgean goal is a "mystic city;" the poet is on a high mountain overlooking the sea. Invoking the aid of Fable and Legend, above the ruined Pillars of Hercules, the Lost Atlantis, and the undiscovered Eldorado, he seeks the fabled wonders of Timbuctoo. A priestess shows the way and a bright Seraph, not unlike the glorified A.H.H., permits that "vast circumference of thought" until he actually sees a "wilderness of spires, and chrystal pile/Of rampart upon rampart, dome on dome." But, like the apotheosis of *In Memoriam*, pierced through with doubt, the young poet doubts the "similitude" of his description, his present mind is clouded by "indecision" and the celebrated Tennyson dubiety is introduced—"if I saw / These things distinctly, for my human brain / Stagger'd beneath the vision, and thick night / Came down upon my eyelids, and I fell." The spirit of Fable raises him up, but confesses that soon the Spirit of Discovery (scientific knowledge) will darken the city of dreams and diminish it to a mere mud-walled, barbarian settlement. Just as later, on the Rectory lawn, the youth was left alone and "all was dark!"

The Devil and the Lady, with uncharacteristo gusto, nevertheless explores many of the subjects he was to draw upon during his long poetic career: The Devil becomes the voice of despair in "The Two Voices," the young wife bent upon adultery is an early study of the late adulterous Queen Guinevere, the Magus is the elderly figure he will use for narrative point of view in Merlin, Ulysses, Tithonus, the Northern Farmer, Lucretius, Tiresias, the Ancient Sage, the octogenarian exile from Lockesley Hall, and many more. "The Coach of Death" 1823, is an early version of "The Vision of Sin" 1842. And the verbal similarities are unmistakable between "Perdidi Diem," written when he was in his teens:

> A carcase in the coffin of this flesh,
> > Pierc'd thro' with loathly worms of utter Death
> My soul is but th' eternal mystic lamp,
> Lighting that charnel lamp,
> Wounding with dreadful days that solid gloom,
> And shadowing forth th' unutterable tomb,
> Making a "darkness visible"
> Of that which without thee we had not felt
> As darkness, dark ourselves and loving night,
> Night-bats into the filtering crevices
> Hook'd clinging, darkness-fed, at ease:
> Night-owls whose organs were not made for light.

***

and "Happy-the Leper's Bride" written when Tennyson was eighty:

VII

. . . body is foul at best.

VIII
The fairest flesh at last is filth on which the worm will
        feast
This poor rib-grated dungeon of the holy human ghost,
IX
This Satan-haunted ruin, this little city of sewers
This wall of solid flesh that comes between your soul and
        mine

Tennyson's perennial fear of death "the loathly worms of utter Death" is continued two years later, in "The Supposed Confessions of a Second-Rate Sensitive Mind" (which was suppressed by the poet for fifty years and only in 1884 included in the complete edition of the Laureate's works).

. . . On his light there falls
A shadow; and on his native slope,
Where he was wont to leap and climb,
Floats from his sick and filmed eyes,
And something in the darkness draws
His forehead earthward, and he dies.

. . . and the busy fret
Of that sharp-headed worm begins
In the gross blackness underneath.

"The Supposed Confessions" also raise issues recurring in all the Laureate's admired poems. There is the problem of a "common faith" to which he cannot give total commitment; in spite of his great poetic gifts, does he have only a "second-rate . . . mind?" His mother prayed earnestly "Bring this lamb back into thy fold," but how effective was prayer in her union with the epileptic, alcoholic, passionate and depressive Rector of Somersby? Now deceased is she simply "clay?"—Question he will raise again with great urgency in *In Memoriam* for seventeen years after the death of Arthur Hallam. His doubt stems not from pride—"the sin of devils"—but from weakness, indecision and uncertainty, leaving the twenty-seven year old son castigating only himself:

O weary life! o weary death!
O spirit and heart made desolate!
O damned vacillating state!

Chapter II

ೞ)ೞ

Dramatic Monologue, the Soliloquy, and the Stage

The relationship between the dramatic monologue and the soliloquy is entirely obvious. Forsaking the world and the theatre pit, the protagonist speaks to himself, to the audience, or to God.

Robert Browning, justly acclaimed for some of the best poetic monologues of the Victorian Age, seems always to have approached through psychology. As Gilbert Keith Chesterton epigrammatically proclaimed: Browning was continually engaged in the defense of indefensible men. Thus a forensic tone emerges: You may think that I (Duke of Ferrara, Sludge the Medium, Bishop of St. Praxed) am entirely a villain. But I want to show you the way I really am, the way I see, the way I act. The argument is often outrageous—"My Last Duchess"—but always compelling and occasionally persuasive.

Alfred Tennyson, on the other hand, writing almost as many (one fifth of his total production) dramatic monologues as Browning, enters the genre through the gates of philosophy, theology, pathology, geology, astronomy, and evolution. This perhaps masks his employment of the genre and permits the reader to maintain the pleasant illusion that the Laureate's poetry is always lyrical and never dramatic.

But the label of the genre itself unmasks the illusion. To put it flatly, "dramatic" is rooted in drama, and the monologue must present a single soul baring that soul in speech, to an unbelieving jury of peers. Just as radio requires more imagination on the part of the listener than the total submersion of television with its only slight requirement that viewer-listener shall be a part of the creative task, so the dramatic monologue makes a more clamant demand upon the reader than the soliloquy on the stage: — although the goal is essentially the same. In both cases the author presents a fictive character, necessarily tinged with himself, who, through actor or literary personae, fights publicly for his very life. The *Six Characters in Search of an Author*, by Pirandello, reveal to us the agony and compulsion with which they speak. By stage tradition, at the critical crisis of his *agon*, the protagonist separates himself from the other actors, looks up toward the Lights, and lays bare his inner motives. The stage convention is that only he hears his self-appeal, or God hears, but neither the other actors nor the audience hears. It is the alone to the Alone in the theatre—central, compelling, and passionate.

The dramatic monologue, on the other hand, is clothed only by the inner eye of the reader, the tone is provided only by the inner ear, but there is the implicit agreement that this will be known by all who read. The tangents form a non-equilateral triangle from author through character to reader, who then returns his personal-cultural reading of the character to author by self-referent clues. The persons involved, author and reader, necessarily invest the character with their own personalities (psychology) and ideas (philosophy). Therefore the fixedness of the characters is vastly different from the fluidity of an author who changes while he writes and a reader who changes while he reads. The theatrical audience is always instructed and confined by voice, gesture, costume, personality of the actor; whereas the monologue page sets the readership free to imagine many permutations. Sir Walter Scott, in *Ivanhoe*, may have in mind a Saxon blonde Rowena who can marry the hero, and a Hebraic brunette who cannot. On the page the reader has the freedom, according to his own experiences and preferences, to transfer the coloring entirely. On the stage the audience is stuck with the visual imagery provided by Director and Stage Manager.

The challenge of the dramatic monologue form resides in its power to persuade. The difficulty resides in the proper balance between the personality of the author, the vividness of character delineation, and that relevance to readers that produces identification, persuasion, or at least consideration. For as private a Poet Laureate as Tennyson, the attraction was great. He could always claim the sentiments expressed were those of the monologue Speaker and not the Author; the readership is always free to respond as private persons or as citizens within a particular culture, race, or religion.

Tennyson began his monologues so early, 1830, that he is obviously relying upon the idyll tradition of Classical Greece, Theophrastian characters, or the soliloquy tradition of the Jacobean stage, rather than any reliance upon the later, masterful monologues of his younger contemporary, Robert Browning. Printed among his *juvenilia*, "Supposed Confessions of a Second Rate Sensitive Mind" almost gives the whole technique away by its title: Why are these confessions only "Supposed" and not "Genuine?" "Confessions" traces the genre to St. Augustine, Dante, and the Catholic Confessional booth as well as the Evangelical "mourning bench." "Second-Rate" by comparison with whom? "Sensitive" is clearly in the pejorative mode among nineteenth century British males, rather than the laudatory mode of its current use by feminists.

The psychological profusion of the title would have set Browning to showing us a young man, comfortable in the knowledge of his failings, seeking to convince the reader that these failings simply mark him as a man, and human. Tennyson projects agony rather than complacent self-acceptance. There are no less than four major antagonists in the poem:

a. The Evangelical background reminds him repetitiously that Christ died for him and that his self-willfulness becomes one of the "thorns that girt Thy brow."
b. His clergyman-fathered mother with "mild deep eyes upraised, that knew / The beauty and repose of faith." She represents that "common faith" that neither questions nor rebels—thus it can be expressed in beauty and repose.
c. But the animal world convinces him that there is something in nature which draws the lamb's head earthward in death, and after?—the almost indescribable horror of "the busy fret / Of that sharp-headed worm begins / In the gross blackness underneath." Thus even in his early youth the poet was exposing that special vulnerability to death that would motivate him for seventeen years of its full-flowering in the agony of loss for Arthur Hallam.

    d. The last antagonist is least expressed in the poem, yet produces
the "damned vacillating state" that makes him doubtful of
his mental acuity and uncertain of his own identity.
[Browning's protagonists never doubt their intellectual
capacity or the continuity of identity]

> I am too forlorn,
> Too shaken: my own weakness fools
> My judgment, and my spirit whirls
> Moved from beneath with doubt and fear.

This final antagonist is rooted in an Augustan truism: "It is man's privilege
to doubt." But Tennyson does not exercise it with pleasure or self-
righteousness. It does not provide him with an "Anchor" for his "frailty."
It precisely delineates an anchor that lures but does not hold, and which
ends only by underlining his "frailty." A "weary life" will be followed
by "weary death" resulting in the present condition of "spirit and mind
made desolate."

    Here is no boastful self-sufficiency of Count Guido, exercising high
marital rights in Browning's *The Ring and the Book*. Here is only the
poor priest Caponsacchi, eternally torn between human compassion for
Pompilia and his clerical vows to God. Which is more essentially dramatic,
the Aristotelian activism of the husband pursuing his wife and inflicting
wounds which will bring her to death's door, or the interior struggle
within a priest who aids a wife's escape from an abusive husband in
violation of his church's policy not to interfere in domestic altercations?
As the nineteenth century focuses attention on interior rather than exterior
drama (*The Haunted Mind: The Supernatural in Victorian Literature*,
eds. Robert Haas, Elton Smith), we are led to estimate the balance of
physical abuse, pursuit, and wounding against the bleeding conscience of
the hapless and perhaps heroic priest. Browning does make an emphasis
Tennyson seems uninterested in. No multi-faceted appeal to half Rome,
the *Tertium Quid*, even the Papacy, which have the effect of fracturing
the social consensus. Tennyson calls in no such jury of multi-verse
citizens. The canvas is much smaller and, therefore, much more intense.
One person caught in toils of conscience and seeking a personal solution.

    Tennyson has been much admired for his Classical dramatic
monologues. The one which might have been written by Browning is
surely "Ulysses." The Jacobean *superbia* of Ulysses and his immense

self-confidence are surprising amidst Tennysonian soul-searching. First published in 1842, the author recalled its genesis at shortly after the tragic death of Hallam in Vienna, 1835. The narrative structure of the poem of course, comes from Homer's *Odyssey*, but the mood was surely derived from Dante's *Inferno*, Canto 26:

> "O brothers," said Ulysses to his mariners, "who through a thousand perils have reached the West, to this so little vigil of your senses that remains be ye unwilling to deny the experience, following the sun, of the world that hath no people. Consider ye your origin; ye were not made to live as brutes, but for pursuit of virtue and knowledge."

Having spent twenty years at the Trojan War, he finds his wife "aged," himself "idle," his country composed of "barren crags," the citizens of Ithaca a "savage race, / That hoard, and sleep, and feed, and know not me." After this long absence could they be expected to know their king? But secure in his self-knowledge, Ulysses boasts that he is a roamer, honored in all the places he has visited. As for his son Telemachus, surely it is now his turn to roam "with a hungry heart" and "win honor" everywhere. But the self-centered father claims priority for himself and dismisses the faithful son as just the one to do Ulysses' proper task, "by slow prudence to make mild / A rugged people." With an unpaternal farewell sneer he dismisses his son and returns to his own all-important itinerary: "He works his work, I mine." He has already measured his son's capacity as "blameless . . . in the sphere of common duties." He can depend on the lad to "pay / Meet adoration to my household gods."

Strictly Tennysonian are the antitheses of the poem. Return from wandering to begin, after only three seasons, a new wandering. Youth left behind (Telemachus), aged mariners "smite / The sounding furrows" to "seek a new world." Morning is the proper hour for new adventuring, but this crew departs when "The long day wanes" and "the slow moon climbs." Fresh enterprise should be of eastern direction, but Ulysses sails westward "beyond the sunset . . . until I die." Making landfall at the Happy Isles they may visit the "great Achilles." But the address is faulty—he is dead and only the departed visit the Land of Shades. Civic duty in Ithaca is evaded by one who "cannot rest from travel." Leaving the Greek rocks of Ithaca, Penelope the faithful wife, Telemachus the dutiful son, they will push off even though the gulfs may "wash us down."

Only the last line is so Browningesque that authorship might seem in question:

> . . . strong in will
> To strive, to seek, to find, and not to yield.

So a dramatic monologue full of the longing to escape land for sea, evade civic duty, slip the bounds of family union, ends up by assuring British imperialists that they should continue exploration, seizure of foreign lands, and never, never let them go!

Just as "Ulysses" (1842) is epic drama—the death of kings and the rise and fall of empires, so "Tithonus" (1860) is mythic dramatic monologue in narrative form. There is astonishingly little about the gods in "Ulysses," still full of unabated ardor for new experience and the fulfillment of his world reputation for wily maneuvering:

> I am become a name
> For always roaming with a hungry heart."

The two monologues are full of passionate life, barely concealing a deep wish for death. In the former it is the violent death of the hero and his aging crew; in the latter the weary death of a man tired by the demands of godhood:

> those dim fields about the homes
> Of happy men that have the power to die
> And grassy barrows of the happier dead.

Ulysses "strove with gods;" Tithonus, lifted by Aurora to surrogate godhood, longed to be an ordinary man:

> Why should a man desire in any way
> To vary from the kindly race of men?

So the two monologues move in opposite directions: the heroic human exulting in his struggles with gods, and the god-adopted man who wishes only to be human. Since a cardinal aspect of the dramatic monologue is the dilemma of the writer expressed through actors' masks, the forty-three year old poet seems to feel no lessening of his creative thrust for supremacy, while only eighteen years later he is sinking beneath the weight of *vates* or Laureate to a nation. However the second mood cannot be taken too seriously when we recall that the Laureate, between 1875 and 1892 (aged sixty-six to eighty-three) launched an "epic history" of England in seven plays!

The voice of the protagonist in "Ulysses" is unvaryingly heroic; in "Tithonus" it varies from the self-pity of "A white-hair'd shadow" with "cold wrinkled feet" to the stentorian rejection of "I earth in earth forget these empty courts!" Appropriately the prosody is in perfect harmony with the mood of the monologuist.

We begin with the damp decay of which Tennyson is the acknowledged master:

> The woods decay, the woods decay and fall,
> The vapors weep their burthen to the ground.
> Man comes and tills the field and lies beneath,
> And after many a summer dies the swan.

But what Alexander Pope might have called the "soft strain of Camilla" is immediately followed by the Ajax hammering in the furious spondaic outbreak:

> Me only cruel immortality
> Consumes

With a strong accent on almost every syllable, the outburst establishes a pattern of outrage spat out of a furious heart.

Of course the next passage telling the mythic story of Aurora and Tithonus is elegant, rejoicing in the excitement of the son of King Laomedon chosen by the goddess of the dawn: "So glorious in his beauty and thy choice." But when the Hours grant immortality but not eternal youth the Ajax fury returns:

> . . . thy strong Hours indignant work'd their wills
> And beat me down, and marr'd and wasted me,
> And tho' they could not end me, left me maim'd
> To dwell in presence of immortal youth,
> Immortal age beside immortal youth,
> And all I was in ashes.

Once again the accents clang and clash with unbridled fury.

The next two passages, full of splendid sensuosity, give the Victorian version of Olympic coitus: Aurora's cheek reddens, her bosom heaves, her sweet eyes brighten. But even this rhapsodic awakening is broken by harsh Ajax hammering: the wild team which loves Aurora will "blind the stars," and "beat the twilight into flakes of fire." This is simply the goddess' preparation for her day's work. But when she returns from her orbit across the heavens, clamant for love, Tithonus:

> . . . felt my blood
> Glow with the glow that slowly crimson'd all
> Thy presence and thy portals, while I lay,
> Mouth, forehead, eyelids, growing dewy-warm
> With kisses balmier than half-opening buds
> Of April, and could hear the lips that kiss'd
> Whispering I knew not what of wild and sweet

The rich and sensuous seduction in the sky is followed by a simple domestic scene on earth. Happiness is no longer kisses wild and sweet, it is instead the power to die! Men are happy because there is a built-in termination to mortality; even happier are the corpses already lying beneath "grassy barrows."

Then the tone once again abruptly shifts to the sharp-edged peremptory. "Release" me, "Restore" me to the ground. In your morning orbit, glowing with beauty, you can look down on my grave, while I, decaying to earth, can "forget these empty courts" and ever-young Aurora demanding passion from a tired old man.

Obviously it is possible to read only about gentle decay, sensuous passion, god-like love and thus decide this is the *lyrical* Tennyson. But this is to ignore the peremptory cry for release, the outrage of aging immortality, the beating and marring and wasting of the jealous Hours— in other words, the very outcries that make this a *dramatic* monologue, not a lyrical song. Browning's protagonists will shock, explain, and persuade; Tennyson's will demand and tear acquiescence from the reading audience.

"Locksley Hall" (1842) was published in the same collection as "Ulysses" after the ten-year poetic silence 1833-1842. A long philosophical monologue within a Victorian frame (a hunt with comrades), it starts with mordant self-pity, moves into jealous accusation, and climaxes in a hopeful prophecy—"Forward, forward let us range" marred only by an ugly curse upon the Hall: Let the woods wither, let the roof-tree fall in, let thunder, rain, hail, fire, snow fall on the unoffending edifice; the protagonist has bidden farewell, and with a mighty wind, he roars seaward.

Biographically the poet had reason for complaint. Although son of a first-born son, his father was rejected and a younger son made heir. In 1833 his best friend died untimely and financial difficulties made it necessary for Tennyson to delay marriage to Emily Sellwood from 1836-1850. His own attempts (by pyroglyphs) to rescue the family financially were resounding failures. He might well have suffered from a sense of great talent rejected by a materialistic society and personal fate.

It is difficult to read "Locksley Hall" without consideration of the ways the monodrama *Maud* (1855), the generic medley *The Princess* (1847), and the great elegy *In Memoriam* (1850) fill out the themes barely sketched in the dramatic monologue. The first section of "Locksley Hall" is a passionate complaint of how family members wound each other and reject each other and how a materialistic social order weights gold above love and talent. The second section supplies a one-sided and inadequate model for the battle of the sexes, later to be revised and corrected in *The Princess*. The concluding passages of the monologue assess the Victorian world and its possible future, just as *In Memoriam* became a compendium of science, biology, geology, politics, theology, and religion.

> Tennyson more than any other writer of his day interpreted the Victorian Age to itself. . . . . Tennyson was keenly sensitive to the movements of the time . . . politics . . . social reform . . . the new science . . . the disquieting doctrine of evolution." (F.J.C. Hearnshaw, *Spectator*, Oct. 6, 1917, p. 352)

The basic problem of the protagonist is his jealous and spiteful response to the rejection by his affianced cousin, and more particularly, by her family. "Shallow-hearted," "Puppet to a father's threat," obediently rejecting the superior suitor (him!) and settling for a "range of lower feelings and a narrower heart" (the man she marries). Written, like *Maud* in the Spasmodic style, he luxuriates in the obedient wrong done to him by the one he passionately loves. Cursed be "social wants," "social lies," "sickly forms," and especially "the gold that gilds the straiten'd forehead of the fool!"

Admitting that all of this was "blustering," yet he egotistically insists he would have loved her "more than ever wife was loved." The author, with a father sometimes considered insane by his parishioners, his wife and his children, with a brother who spent time in an asylum, now asks "Am I mad?" in the Spasmodic tones of Alexander Smith and Sydney Dobell.

Then the protagonist takes revenge upon his faithless cousin. "I am shamed thro' all my nature to have loved so slight a thing," in the accents of every youth who denigrates the worth of the girl who rejects his suit. From Amy to all women, the protagonist blusters on: "Nature made them blinder motions bounded in a shallower brain." What is any woman?

> Woman is the lesser man, and all thy passions, match'd with mine,
> Are as moonlight unto sunlight, and as water unto wine —

And so the great master of metaphor commits a metaphoric crime because of the sting of his wound not so much to his heart as to his ego. Clearly such a definition of woman needs confession, repentance, and correction, now put into the lips of the Prince in *The Princess* (1847). The new definition drops foolish metaphors and quite sensibly states its axiom:

> Woman needs man to achieve womanhood;
> Man needs woman to achieve manhood;
> Therefore, in love they are equal
> (*The "Two Voices"* Elton Smith, page 43).

"Locksley Hall" also anticipates the wide-ranging examination of the Victorian world found in its completeness only in *In Memoriam*. The dramatic monologue recalls the nights spent watching the "Pleiads," the boyish days spent by the sea entranced by geology and evolution—those "fairy tales of science." Men are his brothers in the "Parliament of man, the Federation of the world." They work together toward an extraordinary future in which humans will control the skies, airplanes dropping "costly bales" of goods or in international warfare raining the "ghastly dew" of bomb and gas—"the nations' airy navies grappling in the central blue," until common sense leads the nations to eschew wars on the kindly earth.

But Amy's rejection still cuts and bleeds, making it difficult for the protagonist who hunts solutions instead of deer. He considers dropping out of the white race:

> I will take some savage woman, she shall rear my dusky race.

***

Iron-jointed, supple-sinew'd, they shall dive, and they shall run,
Catch the wild goat by the hair, and hurl their lances in the sun;
Whistle back the parrot's call, and leap the rainbows of the brooks,
Not with blinded eyesight poring over miserable books —

He knows he is thinking like a fool, that his words are wild. With his Eurocentric elitism,

. . . I count the grey barbarian lower than the Christian child.

What? "herd with narrow foreheads," mate "with a squalid savage"?

But even in Europe he cannot sustain his sanguine vision of nations uniting to eliminate war. There is another kind of armed conflict, class against class, the hungry against the well-fed: "Slowly comes a hungry people, as a lion, creeping nigher." So the narrator can only settle for the weak affirmations of the poet: "Yet I doubt not thro' the ages one increasing purpose runs."

Gone the bluster, ended the self-pitying complaints, the lure of lower cultures, the excitement of railroad and airships. Left only with the negative-affirmative comment "I doubt not."

We have examined three great Tennyson dramatic monologues; mythic ("Tithonus"), Classical ("Ulysses"), contemporary ("Locksley Hall"). The rhetorical elements of the egotistical sublime, rage and rejection, and emotional wounding are sufficient to show, in this small sampling of a major Tennyson genre, that they are markedly, even stridently "dramatic" as well as solepcistic.

Soliloquy

Just as the dramatic monologue constitutes one fifth of Tennyson poetry, one might expect the inward moving soliloquy to be a major constituent of his drama. But such is not the case. We will examine several remarkable soliloquies for their own sakes. We will also discover that many of his soliloquies are forms of Exposition to introduce the stage audience to the dramatic situation, or interrupted soliloquies broken by a listener, or soliloquies of remembrance of past experiences, or personal credoes (like Shakespeare's Iago).

It is also surprising that the pen which wrote *In Memoriam* and *Idylls of the King* or *Queen Mary* (longer than Shakespeare's *Hamlet*) should write such comparatively brief soliloquies as if Tennyson doubted his ability to control the unruly pit through a lengthy personal exposition. Indeed we know the prose drama *The Promise of May* was interrupted frequently during the soliloquies about naturalistic philosophy and modern man's freedom from ethical constraints, the most celebrated of which were shouted by the Marquis of Queensbury.

Queen Mary (1875) has at least five major soliloquies. Act III, Scene ii, Mary feels movement within her womb and exultantly whispers "He hath awaked! He hath awaked! / He stirs within the darkness!" This arrival will thaw Philip's bleakness, she muses. The child will be a second Defender (after his father and grandfather) of the Catholic Church and will quell the supporters of Princess Elizabeth and quench the Reformation's light. Luther and Zuinglius can now return to Hell. Heresy dead, faith living: "The King is here! My star, my son!" Sir Ralph Bagenhall presents the position of the Protestant opposition: "We strove against the papacy from the first": William the Conqueror, Edward I, Henry II, but now Spain has triumphed. "I am ashamed that I am Bagenhall, English" (III, iii).

Princess Elizabeth dreams of being a common "milkmaid," but she is still Harry's daughter, Gardiner's obstacle, and at night she dreams:

> How oft the falling axe, that never fell,
> Hath shock'd me back into the daylight truth
> That it may fall today!

Archbishop Cranmer, headed for the headman's axe, repents that "Disgraced, dishonor'd — not by them indeed, / By mine own self — by mine own hand!" (IV, ii).

But the first and last words in soliloquies rightfully belongs to Mary. The first (I, v) brings a vision of Lady Jane Grey's coming execution. A traitor, yes, but only a child victimized by her family's ambition. Womanlike, she realizes that her head which will fall is "So full of grace and beauty!" Would that hers were so lovely! She wishes beauty for Philip's sake — eleven years her junior. Even "the bastard sprout" Elizabeth is far fairer than Mary. Will Philip find her attractive? Mary and Philip are alike in the multitude of their enemies: Bishop Gardiner, the Council, Parliament, the British people. But Mary has always been little loved:

> My hard father hated me;
> My brother rather hated me than loved;
> My sister cowers and hates me

So she spits out her litany of hate. But with Philip by her side, they two

> . . . will lead
> The living waters of the Faith again
> Back thro' their widow'd channel here.

So from jealousy of other's beauty, anger at the rejection of Philip by her people, through a Litany of hatred for a father's hardness, a brother and half-sister's hatred, she melts into an idyllic future restoration of England to the true Faith—all of which the audience knows will not happen, ideals and dreams that fade away.

Thoughtfully, Mary provided her own epitaph:

> never woman meant so well,
> And fared so ill in this disastrous world (V, ii)

The first soliloquy in *Harold* (1876) comes appropriately from the dying king, Edward the Confessor, full of that evasion of civic duty Tennyson found particularly reprehensible in "Ulysses," "The Lotos Eaters," *Idylls of the King.* The old King admits he, half-Norman, may "love the Norman" architecture ("statelier shrines"), the Norman priesthood ("God speaks through abler voices"), the Norman culture compared with the native Anglo-Saxon ("narrowness and coldness"). In a soliloquy against the background of comets in the heavens and rebellion in the north, Edward takes pride in his life of "utter purity," abstention from sexual relations with his wife, the great church he built, the holy bones he collected, the miracles he has performed—all dependent upon Saxon Harold Godwin who administered the realm and fought its enemies while the King prayed (Act I, scene i).

Scene ii depicts Aldwyth who, unlike Mary's love for Spanish Philip (*Queen Mary*) loves Harold passionately because she desperately desires to be Queen of England. She dismisses the pale devotion of Edith ("She hath but love enough to live, not love"). By political alliance she will join the sons of Godwin and the sons of Alfgar knowing Harold will accept a "scapegoat marriage" for the sake of "England's wholeness." A strong character, Aldwyth plays the role of villainess with zestful lack of compunction.

In Harold's soliloquy torn between battle ardor ("some wide waste field / With nothing but my battle axe and him / To spatter his brains") and self-loathing because he was tricked and pressured into swearing support for William the Norman's claims to the English throne upon the bone-relics of the Norman saints. A craven and a liar, he was betrayed by love of his brother Wulfnoth—to which captive Wulfnoth replies "Forgive me, brother, I will live here [in William's prison as royal hostage] and die" (II, ii). It is notable that in every way the diction is bleaker and more brutal (Dark Ages) than that of *Queen Mary* (Middle Ages).

The chief soliloquy in the "epic drama" of the last Saxon king, is uttered by Harold after a series of visions. Edward, Wulfnoth, and Tostig each prophesy that although he won at Stamford Bridge, he will die on Senlac Hill. Even the Norman Saints impressively appear against him:

> O hapless Harold! King but for an hour!
> Thou swarest falsely by our blessed bones,
> We give our voice against thee out of Heaven!

Thus Harold's final soliloquy (V, i) becomes a series of replies to each accusation. Yes, I will die by the arrow of which Edward's spirit warned me. "I die for England then, who lived for England — /What nobler?" To Tostig he replies that he left South England unprotected in order to fight against Tostig in the North. Thus "The Norseman's raid / Hath helped the Norman." So Godwin's descendants killed off their whole family line. To the Norman Saints he confesses his "self-disdain" for swearing falsely over their "gilded ark of mummy-saints." His excuse is that "I knew not that I sware." His condition is facing his last great battle, knowing in advance that he will perish and the war be lost.

When Tennyson wrote *Becket* (1879), he dedicated the play to the Lord Chancellor, Earl of Selborne, calling it a "dramatic memorial of your great predecessor" meanwhile admitting that although it was "dramatic," it was "not intended in its present form to meet the exigencies of our modern theatre." Nevertheless it provided Henry Irving with one of his greatest roles and became very successful on the stage, both in England and America. Just as Harold's soliloquy followed a four-fold dream, Thomas à Becket's soliloquy came to him in the form of a dream, so that instead of Becket unburdening himself to God only, God addressed him only.

Henry II, having already given the Lord Chancellorship of England to his youthful comrade, now sought to force upon him the high office of Archbishop of Canterbury. In shocked reaction to the dual office and strong reaction to his own unworthiness, Becket had responded "Am I the man?" (Act I, scene i). Now the question comes from him again, in his sleep, this time addressed to God. Look at me, I love wine, delicate meats, secular splendours, actors, dogs, hawks, apes, lions, lynxes. And God replies: "Thou art the man, and all the more the man." Becket explains carefully what God must already have known: Henry is my best friend; all my political advancement I owe to him. He will expect me to support the ancient powers of the Throne over the Church. And God replies: "Thou art the man and all the more the man." Then having drawn Becket close in an embrace, He "smote me down upon the minster floor./ I fell."

So, at the play's beginning, Tennyson plants the tragic omens: the King's friend, the Church's archbishop—smitten and falling. Less than being heroic in deed, he has become the King's Pawn and God's Pawn, just as the play begins with a chess game which Becket wins, then becomes an ecclesiastical game Henry wins, and only finally, at long last, a game the martyred archbishop wins only from Heaven.

In a second, more agonized soliloquy (I, i), sending Rosamund back to her protected Bower, and the Great Seal of England back to the King who gave it, Becket agonizes over a position that places him as Chancellor *beneath* Henry and as Archbishop *over* Henry: "The worldly bond between us is dissolved, / Not yet the love." At the end awaits martyrdom.

Henry too experiences agony:

> My comrade, boon companion, my co-reveller
> The master of his master, the King's king (I, iii).

As Chancellor-Archbishop, along with his best friend Henry, they might have ruled England together. But now that he has chosen the Church over the Throne, he has become "False to himself, but ten-fold false to me!"

One of the most interesting soliloquies of the drama is delivered by Eleanor, Countess of Aquitaine, Queen to monk Louis of France, mother of kingly sons, "I that thro' the Pope divorced King Louis . . . I that wedded Henry." Her entire appeal is to authority. She brought Aquitaine to Henry; she fought by his side to make him King, she (by contrast with Rosamund) is his properly wedded wife. They both bore him sons; but only hers are legitimate. A strong portrait of a strong woman, shaper of the Age of Courtly Love, she stands in the great tradition of monarchs and troubadours.

The Falcon (1879), a one-act play, and *The Cup* (1880), a two-act play ran on the stage for sixty-seven and one hundred thirty nights respectively. Although brief in length there are a couple of memorable soliloquies. Count Federigo's ode to his last and best friend, his falcon, is full of Hopkinsian hyperbole of praise: "princess of the cloud," "plumed purveyor," "far-eyed queen of the winds." Built about an O. Henry twist so that the prized bird which the Lady desires for her sick son, is served her for a lunch she does not desire. Lonely and loveless, the speaker equates his condition with that of the bird, mateless and of a dying breed.

"Pines, beech and plane," the villain Synorix sees about him, remembering a maiden he glimpsed three years earlier when he was removed as tetrarch for his unbridled behavior with the women of Galatia. Now returned as that province's king, he plots to accuse her husband of treason against Rome and thus make Camma his queen. The symbol is the late Diana cup of a many-breasted fertility goddess instead of the earlier cup of the chaste goddess Artemis.

The Promise of May (1882), Tennyson's only prose drama, like *The Cup*, describes the deterioration of morals in a culture, ancient or modern. Edgar's opening soliloquy is more like the lecture of a cultural historian than the impassioned cry of a human caught in the toils. The villain Edgar meditates on what a help it has been to him to think of man as a Lockean or Godwinian "automatic series of sensations" (Act I). If man lives only by and for sensations (the utilitarianism of Jeremy Bentham and John Stuart Mill), he ought always to choose the pleasantest (choose pleasure, not pain—the New Hedonism). So in this innocent, rural landscape, he hopes "to crop the flower [Eva]" and pass on unheeding to her pregnancy and public disgrace.

> And if my pleasure breed another's pain,
> Well — is not that the course of Nature, too?

almost restating Darwin's doctrine of the survival of the fittest and the need for struggle to produce the hearty species.

Having given a clear lecture on the amoralities he observes, Edgar (now heir of his uncle's estate) moves "in the iron grooves of Destiny" (perhaps making the same error about the shape of train tracks that

Tennyson made in "Locksley Hall"). Since man's life is "A willy-nilly current of sensations," why should he ever feel remorse for past pleasure? "Reaction must needs follow revel." He calls Nature "a liar, making us feel guilty / Of her own faults." Genetically speaking, his grandfather was a womaniser; why not the grandson, too? He challenges John Locke— "a poor philosopher who call'd the mind / Of children a blank page, a *tabula rasa*." Edgar's experience has taught him the inevitability of genetic inheritance (the direction in which we seem to be moving at the close of the twentieth century).

> There, there, is written in invisible inks
> Lust, Prodigality, Covetousness, Craft,
> Cowardice, Murder — and the heat and fire
> Of life will bring them out (II)

It should be of no surprise that the Free-thinkers in the audience rose in a tumult!

Tennyson's last play, *The Foresters*, was written in 1870, published in 1881, but not performed until March 17, 1892 — the same year the playwright died on October 6. The first and second acts contain two soliloquies on Robin Hood's birthday: the first brief and cheerful (iii), the second long, darker and more foreboding (II, i).

Maid Marian has accepted his ring and a single kiss, but stipulates there will be no wedding until her brother is ransomed from the Holy Land Crusade. If a birthday celebrates the passing of a year, why should we make merry? If it indicates the beginning of a new year, then it is full of Hope, like Spring, the sap rising, the bud bursting. So "Strike up a song, my friends, and then to bed."

The second soliloquy is in obedience to his deceased mother who urged him "to carve / One lone hour from it [his birthday]" to meditate upon the Last Trumpet and the rising of the dead into eternal life.

He examines his earthly situation: exiled King Richard is safe from bloody battle because he is in prison awaiting the national ransom for his relief. Robin is an outlaw, thief, and king of thieves—but robbing the robbers to give to the robbed. The free forest life suits him better than the groined roof in his ancestral halls which hide the heavens. But if captured, those very eyes would be put out. Unlike the usurper John, he has perfect confidence in his followers. Indeed, to indulge in a pun, the vice of Vice-King John has made Robin "king of all the discontent / Of England."

Friar Tuck delivers a cutting parable "Geese, man!" about the untrustworthiness of absent kings—to the King's very face. And Marian delivers a pithy parable — "Pity, pity!" about hunted and hunter coming to the same doom (IV; I). But her most rousing soliloquy—"No nearer to me! back!" is delivered in ringing tones of defiance to Prince John and the Sheriff of Nottingham. The Prince she accuses of dishonouring "The daughters and wives of your own faction." Caring only for bodies, not souls, he builds his private harem—of which she will not be a part. Should he make her queen over England, she would refuse to mate with

> . . . one that holds no love is pure,
> No friendship sacred, values neither man
> Nor woman save as tools

The Sheriff sought to buy her with gold for her brother's ransom and her father's estate. "Marriage is of the soul, not of the body." He may murder her; he cannot win her. Her love belongs to Robin and his men. Then in an astonishing Credo for a woman in the Victorian Era—" while / I breathe Heaven's air, and Heaven look down on me . . . I remain / Mistress of mine own self and mine own soul"—light years away from "Locksley Hall 's"

> Woman is the lesser man, and all thy passions, match'd with mine,
> Are as moonlight unto sunlight, and as water unto wine —

and even surpassing *The Princess'*

> For woman is not undevelopt man,
> But diverse.

In this final scene of *The Foresters* Maid Marian emerges as the most physically courageous, the most passionately articulate *Person* in the forest!

The second scene of Act III, *The Devil and the Lady*, a fragment, written in 1823, when Tennyson was a youth of fourteen, nevertheless contains several significant soliloquies, one by the Lady, one by the Devil, and most memorably one by the Magus. Written in unrhymed iambic pentameter, it introduces many of the themes the mature Tennyson would explore in dramatic monologues, dramas, and occasional pieces.

The soliloquy begins after the departure of the Devil, with an extended metaphor of a "summer fly" skimming the surface of a deep black pool, with no comprehension of the depths beneath its delicate feet. Man, on the other hand, sees the depth but "plunges madly into it." Even after a night of "crime and care," he still rises to follow the phantom voice of soft temptation.

This is the distinction between Boy and Man. Living in "passionless tranquillity," the Boy's natural mind warms to all the best impressions. But in the Man, "the rude breath of dissipation" hardens into stone. Sea anemones, soft and yielding in the watery depths, become rock hard when long exposed to air.

The Magus retires to a Northern casement of his home where he may look down upon every scene of wild abandonment and hear the faintest whisper of depravity. The "summer fly," the "black pool," and the "seaplant" all anticipate the Laureate's great skill with metaphor. Temptation as a "phantom" raises the question of the reality of evil and the certainty of identity that the poet often tended to dissolve in air. The Wordsworthian sense of the child trailing clouds of glory from his heavenly home gives Platonic support to his theory of the superiority of boys to men.

The meditation upon the wisdom of Nature and the folly of man, the phantom unreliability of being and matter, the stance of the Poet at some "Northern casement" looking down upon the chaotic folly of the world— these are all staggering in view of the Laureate's exploration of precisely the same themes. Well might Bernard Groom claim "no profound changes" in his poetry from beginning to ending. As the Trinity notebook vividly shows, *The Devil and the Lady* presents us with both the schoolboy sketches (illustrations) and scrawls (handwriting) to convey the winged thoughts of a precocious teen-age dramatic genius. He wrote drama at the beginning, he wrote dramatic poems in between, he wrote full-fledged dramas, seven of them, at the ending.

Chapter III

ℰ⤳ℭ

A Play by Any Other Name . . .
The Princess 1847, *Maud* 1855, *Idylls of the King* 1854 (first four), *Enoch Arden* 1864

In *The Many Facèd Glass* 1987, Linda Hughes argues that although we might naturally assume that Tennyson's verse drama emerged from his great dramatic monologues it is more likely that they grew out of the narrative *Idylls of the King* (p. 189ff). Indeed a note in the second volume of the *Memoirs* confesses the poet's longing to print the names of the *dramatis personae* over the "short snip-snap" of their conversation (p.113n). Of course, to have done so would have wreaked violence upon the more contemplative form of the idyll and would have placed the twelve narratives firmly in the dramatic genre. Deplorable from the point of view of the literary purist, but marvelously helpful for the understanding of the reader. However, the focus of emphasis would have subtly shifted from evocation of situation to delineation of character. And the latter was clearly the intention of the laureate in penning lines which were to be delivered on the stage.

Among the many Tennyson works, short or long, which can profitably be seen as dramas rather than simply read as text, *The Princess*, *Maud*, *Idylls of the King*, and *Enoch Arden* are notable. Their range is breathtaking: the first an exploration of the contemporary "woman-problem," the second an extension of the early "spasmodic" declamation of "Locksley Hall," the third the magical rise and tragic fall of the ideal knight and the spiritual kingdom, the fourth the folksy mid-Victorian domestic pastoral of a marriage fractured by shipwreck at sea.

Tennyson called the society-conscious, gender-exploratory poem *The Princess: A Medley*, and in the *Edinburgh Review* Aubrey de Vere defended the sub-title:

> If a man were to scrutinise the external features of our time . . . he would be tempted . . . to give up the task before long, and to pronounce the age a Medley. It would be hard to specify the character of our Philosophy, including as it does all systems, sometimes at open war, and sometimes eclectically combined. In this respect, Mr. Tennyson's poem, *The Princess*, not without design if we may judge by the title, resembles the age, (July-October, 1848, p. 388)

It was certainly the author's intention to correct and compile his earlier comments about the relationship between the sexes, but his "design" is of special interest here. Beginning with a Prologue—the Victorian framing device—recounted by the first person-singular of an un-named visiting Cambridge undergraduate, the drama is contemporized with a strange mingling of Disraeli's "two nations." Working men and their picnicking families attending an outdoor session of their Mechanics Institute, replete with technological demonstrations of fountains, cannon, electricity, a steam-propelled paddle-wheeler, a model railway set, a fire balloon, and telegraphy. By contrast, seven youths, down from Cambridge, are given the grand tour of Vivian-Place with particular reference to the family which had been represented at Agincourt and an ancient chronicle of a female ancestor, a "miracle of noble womanhood"— who could fight like a knight and did not shun "a soldier's death." Workmen, the children of the technologic future; students, of the medieval past. Young Walter Vivian's sister insists that there are thousands of women now alive as noble and dashing as the heroine in the chronicle, "but convention beats them down." She herself hates men for what they have done to women and wishes she were a mighty princess to build a women's college. The un-named narrator is assigned to tell a tale of a princess "six-feet high, / Grand, epic, homicidal"—and he the prince to win her. There follow seven sections, like acts of a play with differing settings interspersed with lyrical songs by the ladies, and ending with a Conclusion to match the Prologue. Like a drama, exposition is followed by rising action sputtering before the demeaning true climax, in a *fausse dénouement*, then a falling action closing with a restoration of order. Not the tragedy of the intrepid knight-in-"drag's" death, but the comedy of a man-hating Patrician scholar who tenderly nurses the fallen male foe and melts completely at the snuggle of a tiny child.

FitzGerald considered *The Princess* to be an example of Tennyson's "old fault of talking big on a common matter" (A. McKinley Terhune, *Life of Edward FitzGerald*, p. 126). Yet John Killham considered the poetic drama to be *Reflections of An Age* (*The Princess*, 1958). The "question of woman," even frothier today than then, challenged Arthur Hugh Clough to write *The Bothie of Tober-na-Vuolich* 1848; Coventry Patmore, *The Angel in the House* 1854-62; Elizabeth Barrett Browning, *Aurora Leigh* 1857. The young visitor to Locksley Hall (1842) considered Amy to be a "puppet," "servile," with "lower feelings and a narrower heart" than his own, woman "the lesser man;" male passions "sunlight" and "wine;" female passions "moonlight" and "water." "Nature made them blinder motions bounded in a shallower brain."

In *The Princess* Tennyson recommends a melodious armistice to the war of the sexes. Each needs the other equally:

> O we will walk this world,
> Yoked in all exercise of noble end,
> And so thro' those dark gates across the wild
> That no man knows. Indeed I love thee: come,
> Yield thyself up, my hopes and thine are one;
> Accomplish thou my manhood and thyself.
>   (VII, 339-344)

So woman "is not undevelopt man" (VII, 259), nor less than man, but "equal" (VII, 285) and "diverse" (VII, 260).

Responding to the urging of his friends, Tennyson bravely wrote a poem about a contemporary social issue. So the Prologue begins with the mingling of the working class heirs of the technological future and Sir Walter Vivian's son's undergraduate friends—heirs of the past. He will clothe the tension in medieval setting and describe an outrageous and heroic woman who will build a woman's college, secure from the temptations and condescension of men. Estimating women, released from societal bondage, as brighter and quicker by far than men, Ida models the curriculum to be just like the great crown colleges of England. But in female garb, the Prince becomes the serpent in this female garden, falls ill and must be nursed, arousing her amorous spirit and witnessing the Princess' surrender to the needs of a little child who aroused her maternal instinct. Thus the restoration of order must establish the genders as equal, diverse, and essential to the fulfillment of each other.

But odd incongruities crop up. The Princess may be an intellectual, but she needs love and motherhood for total fulfillment. The Prince is brave and passionate, but he is also an epileptic who has to be saved from drowning by the competent Princess. Hugh Fausset accused Tennyson of reducing the splendid Princess to a mere *mère de famille*; but in fact, Tennyson was actually at that very time engaged in conversations with John Mitchell Kemble about a projected university for women; so the manipulation is more topical than sentimental. As Charles F.B. Masterman summed it up: Tennyson used the mock-heroic epic form to accomplish for nineteenth century women just what Pope accomplished for the weaker/stronger sex in the eighteenth century—and by the same means—a serio-comic struggle that displays the peculiar strengths and weaknesses of both genders (*Tennyson as a Religious Teacher*, p. 2).

Maud; A Monodrama 1805 may have, as W.J. Rolfe says, arisen out of the song "O that't were possible" printed in *The Tribute* 1837, but the author was clearly anxious to underscore its dramatic quality. Jerome Hamilton Buckley pronounced it to be an example of the Spasmodic Poetry of Sydney Smith and Alexander Dobell. Reading the poem to J.T. Knowles and later to Professor Rolfe, Tennyson explained that this, his favorite dramatic reading, should be called "Maud or the Madness . . . no other poem (a monotone with plenty of change and no weariness) has been made into a drama where successive stages of passion take the place of successive persons . . . I've always said that 'Maud' and 'Guinevere' were the finest things I've written" (W.J. Rolfe, *The Poems of Tennyson*, p. 198). When Dr. Van Dyke called it "a splendid failure," Tennyson replied: "It is dramatic; it is the story of a man who has a morbid nature, with a touch of inherited insanity. . . ."

To consider *Maud* as a "monodrama," explains the hyperbolic extravagance of mood and language, reveals its real shape and form, and prepares the reader for the dramatic climax, the calmer *dénouement* and the patriotic restoration of order. From this critical point of view the three parts become acts and their divisions scenes (much fragmented).

In an article in the *South Atlantic Quarterly* (XLIII), "Tennyson the Psychologist," Roy P. Basler reminds us of Tennyson's own insistence that *Maud* is the "drama" not of a young man falling in love and fighting a duel for his fair lady, but instead the struggle of successive phases of an obsessive passion against each other in a maddened mind.

> Even under fortuitous circumstances the hero might have experienced difficulty in making an adjustment to the "cruel madness of love," for his is essentially an introvertish ego. His dominant wish is to hide, to bury himself in himself. From the time of his father's death his life has been isolated by wish as well as by circumstance, and he resents the return of Maud's family to the neighboring Hall because of an unconscious fear of Maud herself as a source of danger to all that is his. This dominant wish to hide . . . is the essential obsession which throughout the poem marks his reaction to fear and pain, and culminates in Part II in dementia, the diagnostic of which is that he is dead and buried. This introversion is at the root of his attempt to adopt the cynical pose in which he will observe human affairs but not participate in them.

> The plot of the poem, however, is not based primarily upon the conventional love theme as has often been supposed, but rather upon the theme of psychic conflict between the phases of the hero's personality. This view is substantiated by Tennyson's own statement that the poem is a drama of the soul in which "different phases of passion in one person take the place of different characters" (April 1944, 147-148).

With this psycho-analytic key in hand it is possible to read Part I as the spasmodic frenzy of the son of the suicide who looks for release not to science nor poetry, nor the stoicism of either desire or admiration, but to a "passionless peace" especially free from "the madness of love." But instead, twenty-five, he permits himself to fall in love and seek in the seventeen-year-old *Maud* salvation from madness, crime, and a selfish grave. The rest of the psycho-drama moves with crescendoing speed to the fatal duel with Maud's brother, flight from Britain to the Breton coast, return to the "red-ribb'd hollow behind the wood" (Parts I, II), the beloved dead, and his life in tatters. The salvation of the hero comes in jingoistic fashion from the Crimean War (Part III).

However dismaying the solution, the poet has adequately prepared us for the *dénouement*. He has described capitalism as a Schopenhauerian civil war, neighbor looting neighbor, "cheat and be cheated" (I, I, VIII).

War, he proclaims in the first scene, is more heroic than such civil strife which produces violent unrest among the poor, battered wives, adulterated bread, a citizenry sleeping with arms, "Mamonite mothers" who kill their new-born babes to claim the burial-fee, and pharmaceutical prescriptions guaranteed to make the patient worse. Hearing a Quaker preach against war, he insists man is always at war with man, and public foe is healthier than "private blow" (Part II, I). Admitting his personal, psychological handicap:

> My life has crept so long on a broken wing
> Thro' cells of madness, haunts of horror and fear

he boldly asserts that it is nobler to claim Mars for his God, than to worship British millionaires; thus, the public war becomes his personal salvation—"a cause I felt to be pure and true:"

> I wake to the higher aims
> Of a land that has lost for a little her lust of gold,
> And love of a peace that was full of wrongs and shames,
> Horrible, hateful, monstrous, not be told;
> And hail once more to the banner of battle unroll'd!

So the sick protagonist, along with the sick public, have "proved we have hearts in a cause, we are noble still." Decisive public action heals psychic personal ills:

> It is better to fight for the good than to rail at
>   the ill;
> I have felt with my native land, I am
>   one with my kind,
> I embrace the purpose of God, and the
>   doom assign'd. (Part III, V)

Again for Tennyson the solution to private predicament lies in feeling; decisive action is better than private suffering; the poet as soldier is restored to the common run of men—"my kind," and the purpose of God, always unclear, may solve earth's problems by the death of the earthling.

T.S. Eliot claimed that "*Maud* and *In Memoriam* are each a series of poems, given form by the greatest lyrical resourcefulness that a poet has ever shown" (*Essays, Ancient and Modern*, New York: 1936, p. 175ff.).

The formal variety is extraordinary: vituperative declamation, narrative passages, soliloquies and dramatic monologues, meditative musings by the sea, dialogue, and lovely interspersed lyrics like the much admired floral sequence:

> She is coming, my dove, my dear;
>   She is coming, my life, my fate.
> The red rose cries, "she is near, she is near;"
>   And the white rose weeps, "She is late;"
> The larkspur listens, "I hear, I hear;"
>   And the lily whispers, "I wait."

The poet adds that even if he had lain dead for a century, his dust would feel her "airy . . . tread," would "start and tremble" beneath her tread "And blossom in purple and red." One of the striking evidences of how deeply his dramatic poetry is embedded in the non-dramatic works, occurs in the fourth scene of the first part:

> Ah Christ, that it were possible
> For one short hour to see
> The souls we loved, that they might tell us
> What and where they be!

Clearly the passage might as easily be inserted in a canto of Alfred Tennyson's monumental and passionate lament of at least five years earlier for Arthur Henry Hallam, as this passionate cry from a bereft son to his suicide father.

It is ironic that the Tennyson volume that contained *Maud* should also contain "The Charge of the Light Brigade." In the "monodrama," Tennyson uses the Crimean War 1853-1856 between Russia, England, France, Turkey, and Sardinia as the great patriotic event to restore the over-wrought protagonist to social unification and sanity. In the war ballad, the Laureate admits that "some one had blunder'd"—probably the British commander Lord Raglan—and thus a light brigade was foolishly sent to certain extinction by the opposing cannon. War ennobles; war senselessly destroys. A further irony is that the war began between Russia and France for guardianship of the sacred Bible sites in Palestine.

In 1859 appeared the first four *Idylls of the King*: "Enid," "Vivien," "Elaine," and "Guinevere"—studies of medieval ladies a bit like Dante Gabriel Rossetti's later stunning Pre-Raphaelite female portraits. But

Tennyson became interested in *Flos Requm Arthurus* (Joseph of Exeter) long before 1859. "The Lady of Shalott" 1832 was based on the legend Tennyson later (1888) reshaped into the seventh idyll "Lancelot and Elaine." "The Palace of Art," from the same 1832 volume, mentioned the Pendragon's child, or "mythic Uther's deep—wounded son," "Sir Galahad" and "Sir Lancelot and Queen Guinevere" were printed in 1842 at the same time as Tennyson's "Morte d'Arthur," later incorporated into the twelfth idyll, "The Passing of Arthur." However, Edward FitzGerald had heard the "Morte" read from manuscript as early as 1835 (*Memoir*, vol. I, p. 194). Foster's *Life of Landor* records Landor's recollection of hearing the reading of a poem on the subject of the death of Arthur, which he described as "more heroic than any poem of our time, and rivals some of the noblest parts of the Odyssea" (II, p. 323).

This remarkable ability to incorporate poems written twenty-seven years earlier led Arthur Carr to observe:

> Tennyson's later poetry does not break from the pattern of his past. This is why he could revise his early work, as he did for the *Poems of 1842*, with as much grace and tact as if he were still in the midst of writing it for the first time. With thorough integrity he could publish in his later books some poems written long before, and could introduce passages of this early work into poems written a half century later. The persistence of his motives brings his later poetry back to the inescapable themes: in "The Ancient Sage" he returns to the debate of "The Two Voices," in "Lucretius" to the fierce and open warfare between erotic and conscientious impulses, in "Demeter and Persephone" to the ritual of the death and reawakening of nature, in "Crossing the Bar" to the dream voyages of "Morte d' Arthur" and *In Memoriam*, and in his last book to "The Death of Oenone." ("Tennyson as a Modern Poet," *University of Toronto Quarterly*, XIX July 1950, 361-382)

Anyone who considers the *Idylls* from a dramatic point of view is bound to find F.E.D. Priestley's "Tennyson's Idylls," pivotal to the discussion. In 1960, John Killham considered the essay important enough to include in his *Critical Essays on the Poetry of Tennyson* (London, 1960, p. 254 ff). Tennyson himself called the *Idylls* allegories. If the parable dramatizes a simple incident from the common life, an allegory adds to the simple incident a world of symbolic meanings. If Edmund Stedman found them "skillfully wrought of high imaginings, faery spells, fantastic legends, and medieval splendors . . . suffused with the Tennysonian glamor of golden mist" (*Victorian Poets*, Boston, 1903, p. 175),Thomas Carlyle was deeply disappointed by their avoidance of contemporary dilemmas; "inward perfection of vacancy . . . the lollipops were so superlative . . . a refuge from life, a medieval arras" behind which Tennyson hid from the "horrors of the Industrial Revolution" (C.E. Norton, ed., *The correspondence of Thomas Carlyle and Ralph Waldo Emerson*, Boston 1834, II, 339-340). It was Prof. Priestley however who extended Tennyson's allegorical tag to division of the twelve books into groups of four idylls each, thus forming the three acts of a modern play.

Act I opens with the rich symbolism of "The Coming of Arthur" and closes with the crass materialism of "Geraint and Enid." All four of the idylls reach happy endings as parts of the general theme for Act I of order established and good triumphant over evil. Gareth who valiantly overcomes the Star Knights and the Knight of the Castle Perilous, thus proves his own knighthood and serves his King. So Gareth and Lynette serve as human incarnations of the spiritual ideals of Arthur. Geraint and Enid are their dramatic foils, stubbornly following their own will and only reluctantly accepting Arthur's standards. They do not, as yet, represent the recalcitrance of active positive evil, but only the normal resistance before any ideal can become effective in a world of deeds. But there appear some evil omens: the knights are few, some lazy and others mean-spirited. Beyond Camelot, built to music, there stretches the dark and menacing North where Arthur has no sovereignty, his birth is called into doubt and power is exerted only spasmodically by the gallantry of occasional champions. Geraint suspected Enid's fidelity because of a rumor he had heard about Lancelot and the Queen. Amid an atmosphere of social success, but internal contagion, a bridge is thrown to the sagging idealism of Act II.

Act II opens on the grim note of the fratricide of "Balin and Balan" and closes with the spiritual splendor coupled with social deterioration of "The Holy Grail." The rumors about Lancelot-Guinevere have hardened into fact. Weariness of spirit combines with the senile fumblings of an old man after Vivien, to remove "Merlin's white magic" from the equation. Passion and cynicism trap the innocent, pathetic Elaine. The ascetic quest of the knights, coupled with the adulterous passion of the Queen leave Arthur the betrayed master of a barren board and a decimated knighthood.

Act III establishes a bitterly ironic parallel to the Gareth of the second idyll of Act I. Pelleas is as young, eager, and zealous as Gareth, but he seeks to please his lady Ettarre rather than Arthur his King. Instead of the search for the ideal and the life of innocent service, he chooses the harlot Ettarre who cares only for experience. Betrayed both by his cynical lady and his opportunistic best friend, Gawain, the disillusioned knight denies his vows of knighthood and denounces his King. In "The Last Tournament" (re-named in the poem "The Tournament of the Dead Innocence"), Tristram, who repudiates everything the Round Table represents, wins the prize he doesn't care about, presents it to Isolt who doesn't want it, and is stabbed from behind by the cowardly King Mark, her husband.

In "Guinevere," the Queen withdraws from a world which always resists the ideal and King Arthur sets off for a battle which is already lost, in defense of a kingdom which is a hollow shell, ready to collapse upon its own emptiness.

In "The Passing of Arthur" the gloom of the King's defeat and departure is seen as part of that eternal drama in which the Spirit of God incarnates itself intermittently, seeking to make the ideal effective in the recalcitrant world of fleshly matter.

When Tennyson established the order of the idylls, they were to move from early Spring to late Winter, thus providing a Pre-Raphaelite order of seasons and symbols. But it seems, at least to me, that F.E.D. Priestley's organization of the twelve books as the three acts of a modern drama, gives unique meaning and strength to the whole. We finally can see that the sunny friendships of Arthur-Guinevere-Lancelot in Act I, bear within themselves the dark omens of disaster. Act II lets the disaster become apparent, and Act III is torn between an adulterous love of the King's best friend for the King's wife and the inordinate asceticism of the Quest for the Holy Grail. Both forces are inordinate; obsessive passion and world-retreating Quest, so they become the malefactors who create the tragic conclusion. God will continue to seek avatars in the battle of Sense and Soul, but this particular Camelot experiment has gone down the drain.

Enoch Arden 1864, now generally ignored, was one of Tennyson's most popular works. Eugene Parsons, in the pamphlet entitled "Tennyson's Life and Poetry" (2nd ed. 1893), lists twenty-four translations: nine German, two Dutch, one Danish, one Bohemian, eight French, one Spanish, and two Italian—there was even a Latin version by W. Selwyn (London 1867)!

The British Quarterly Review (October 1880) traces the genesis of both *Enoch Arden* and "Aylmer's Field" to the retelling of a friend, who was then requested by the poet, struck by their aptitude for versification, to repeat the tales in writing for his use. The *Memoir* (II, p, 7) both confirms the legend and identifies the friend as Thomas Woolner, the sculptor member of the earliest group of the *P.R.B.*

An "English Idyll," is the salty, fish-smelling tale of a sailor who left his wife in a little shop, and, after being shipwrecked in the tropics, returned to find her wed to another childhood friend. Calculated to please critical friends like grumpy Carlyle, Tennyson was writing about contemporary domesticity and the precariousness of trade and sea-faring. Oddly, Tennyson deliberately applied a lavish, ultra-romantic style to the telling of a simple village yarn, but a basket of fish scarcely loses it characteristic odor by Tennyson's euphemism—"Enoch's ocean-spoil in ocean-smelling osier."

John Ruskin shared Carlyle and Woolner's wish that the laureate should write more about the common life of men in their own generation (*Memoir* I, 453-454), despite his own fondness for the resurrection of Venetian Gothic architecture for Victorian London. About *Idylls of the King*, he mused:

> Treasures of wisdom there are in it, and word-painting such as never was yet for concentration, nevertheless it seems to me that so great power ought not to be spent on visions of things past but on the living present. For one nearer capable of feeling the depth of this poem I believe then would feel a depth quite as great if the stream flowed through things nearer the hearer. . . .

And then, in a rhetorical passage unmatched in most modern critical prose . . .

> . . . I think I have seen faces, and heard voices by road and street side, which claimed or conferred as much as ever the loveliest or saddest of Camelot. As I watch them, the feeling continually weighs upon me, day by day, more and more, that not the grief of the world but the loss of it is the wonder of it. I see creatures so full of all power and beauty, with none to understand or teach or save them. The making in them of miracles and all cast away, for ever lost as far as we can trace, And no "In Memoriam."

At times Tennyson clearly agreed with his friendly critics, as in "Romney's Remorse" 1889—"I have stumbled back again/ Into the common day, the sounder self" (11. 32-33). Richard Monckton Milnes praised Tennyson for moving deliberately away from an "ideal" art of fanciful invention toward a "national" art focused upon immediate actualities (*Life, Letters, and Literacy Remains of John Keats*),

The English idyll does bear striking similarities to *Maud*. High romanticism of passion is shared by both male protagonists; both depart to distant places (Brittany and the Orient), both have more successful rivals, both idylls are climaxed by violence (the duel and the storm at sea), both end in wry acceptance. But *Enoch Arden's* conclusion of consummate domestic bliss shared by his boyhood friend and his former wife and children, was infinitely more acceptable to the British public. Also the tight-lipped Enoch sacrificially withdrawing to save a happy family unit would be more acceptable than a psychotic lover, traumatized by a father's financial debacle and suicide, fighting a melodramatic duel, fleeing to the continent, and throwing himself with relief into the Crimean mess.

Read as a drama, *Enoch Arden* employs its 80 line Exposition of Act I to introduce Enoch, who spoke his love to Annie, whereas Philip loved in silence and lost her. The wedding, birth of a daughter and a son, are all part of the fortunate beginning.

A fall, a broken limb, birth of a sickly son create the obstacles of Act II, which Enoch circumvents only by accepting his former ship-master's offer as boatswain on a "vessel China-bound." Although Annie begs him not to go, with premonitions she will look upon his face no more, he sells his boat, sets her up in a little shop and heroically departs.

Act III details the long wait for the sailor's "wealthy" return. Annie is not a good business-woman because she is not "capable of lies." The weakly second son dies and prosperous Philip begs to serve his two old friends by putting the remaining children in school. Ten years slip by with the children calling their benefactor "Father Philip" and Annie depending upon him for everything. But enough is enough, and when Philip finally urges her to accept her widowhood and his hand in marriage, she begs for one more year, and then they are wed. Another child seals their union and is part of their prosperity.

The fourth Act would trace the ship-wrecked sailor by slow stages back to the harbor from which he sailed and the now-empty house. His garrulous landlady Miriam Lane, unknowing, has told him all the story of his family.

The fifth Act, would show Enoch looking in Philip's window and realizing the happiness of the domestic situation within. The returned wanderer makes his sacrificial vow "Not to tell her, never to let her know," works at odd jobs for a year, then falls into a "Victorian decline" and knows he has only days to live. Fiercely he forces Miriam not to tell his story until he is dead, and only then to bear his blessing to Annie, his daughter, his son, and Philip his old friend. The act would close upon the most lavish and costly funeral the little port had ever seen.

In Plato's *Republic*, the philosopher admits music and mathematics to his ideal city but not drama on the basis that the playwright can dramatize only effeminate heroes who over-react to life's emergencies. The masculine hero, who keeps his own counsel and a tight upper lip clamped upon verbal complaints is essentially non-dramatic, as well as being essentially more British. Thus the protagonist of *Maud*, neurotic and asthenic, given to self-pity and soft self-protection, passionately in love with the sister of his enemy, forced to duel by the insults of that enemy, fleeing to the Continent and returning to find his beloved dead of sorrow— all this, Plato would claim, makes the ideal tragic hero and the worst possible citizen of the ideal Republic.

In this sense, Tennyson chose very intractable material: an ordinary story of village romance, a heroine with three children and a husband away at sea. His claims to heroic standing rest on his willingness to face danger in the support of his family and the silence with which "Enoch Arden *saw.*" This resembles the assignment Wordsworth accepted in Preface to the *Lyrical Ballads* (1800 ed.)—"incidents and situations from common life . . . to relate . . . them . . . in . . . language really used by men . . . to throw over them a certain colouring of imagination . . . and . . . to make these incidents and situations . . . trace . . . the primary laws of our nature. . . ." Nevertheless, the flamboyant hero of *Maud* never becomes a British hero—even when he volunteers for patriotic service in the Crimea. When the poet follows the reverential success of *In Memoriam* by *Maud*, Hugh Fausset tells us the reviewers were so baffled by the change in tone that it was suggested that the "a" or the "u" might be omitted from the title with equal justice (*Tennyson: a Modern Portrait* London 1923, p. iii). But *Enoch Arden*, having a hero and heroine with whom the British public could more easily empathize, immediately went into multiple editions and translations abroad, supplying literature with the "Enoch Arden" theme of the noble but belated hero who returns to his family after they have been happily integrated into a different domestic unit.

Chapter IV

ℰℭ

Three Queens:
Mary, Guinevere, and Victoria

In the previous Introduction and Chapters I and II, we have been dealing with an extraordinary dramatic fragment of *Juvenilia* "The Devil and the Lady," and four major works of the mature poet: *The Princess*, *Maud*, *Idylls of the King*, and *Enoch Arden*. Tennyson called the first a "Medley," suggesting its multi-generic structure of contemporary Mechanics Institute demonstrations, medieval manuscript, aristocratic romance, an ideal women's university, multiple definitions of gender, the strong women/weak male Victorian syndrome, and a number of interspersed songs. When Tennyson subtitled the second "A Monodrama," he opened the door to its consideration as a play. He even specifically indicated that the psychological phases of madness should take the place of the usual *dramatis personae*. In the third, twelve epic books from Arthurian legend, he regretted not being permitted, by generic purists, to print the dialogue as a drama: name of speaker in full capitals, followed by the speech of that dramatic character. The fourth, an "English Idyll" (or a contemporary version of the Arthurian idylls) has a distinct cast of characters and best reveals its progress of meaning by consideration as the acts of a domestic drama.

After the juvenile fragment, when the poet was fourteen his first formal full-length historical drama, *Queen Mary*, was written when the poet was sixty-five, although, as chapter II contended, the dramatic monologues, Arthurian and English idylls, the monodrama, and the medley all qualify, to a limited degree as "dramatic."

In writing on the life of Mary Tudor, Tennyson may well have been planning an extension of Shakespeare's historical dramas. He modestly proposed a trilogy of plays which together would portray the "making of England." *Harold* would describe the impact of Danish raids, Saxon immigration from the continent, and the Norman conquest of 1066. He considered the native peoples as having fallen into a profound "slumber," before the new arrivals created "the greatness of our composite race."

In *Becket* he advanced to the twelfth-century conflict between Thomas à Becket and Henry II to dramatize the British tension between the monarchy and the clergy. *Queen Mary*, first of the plays to be written, was historically the last of the trilogy, meant to celebrate the demise of Roman Catholicism in England and an Anglican-Catholic church at "the dawning of the new age . . . of the freedom of the individual."

The London theatre seemed to be experiencing a renaissance—indeed journalists liked to call it the new Elizabethan age. The domestic Tennyson had long delighted in reading Shakespeare aloud in his deep voice, lengthening out the vowels and diphthongs, but, deciding *Othello* too tragic to be read aloud, put it aside in favor of *Henry IV*—a momentous Rubicon away from tragedy toward chronicle (Thorn, *Tennyson*, p. 431). Thus he was left with history and epic (trilogy), both preferences that shape the major plays.

Two years earlier he had attended the great presentation of Bulwer-Lytton's *Richelieu* and knew of the stage success of W.G. Wills' *Charles the First*. In picking Henry Irving for the rather unrewarding role of Philip II of Spain, he had never seen Irving's *The Bells*, but he witnessed his portrayal of Richelieu, and in March 1874 Irving's triumphant Hamlet—even claiming to have made significant suggestions for Irving's rather unconventional playing of the melancholy Dane. With twenty-three scenes and forty-four characters, Tennyson's *Queen Mary* exceeded in length Shakespeare's *Hamlet*, but came nowhere near the length of Hardy's *Dynasts*.

Of course it had to be cut and the playwright chopped some of the historical scenes so that it became essentially the psychological study of Mary and Philip—a move in surely the right direction, although Professor

Phyllis Grosskurth considered the cuts had produced only "an attenuated psychological study" ("Tennyson, Froude, and *Queen Mary, Tennyson Research Bulletin,* Nov. 1973, ii 44-54). A friend, Mary Brotherton, told Frederick Tennyson that in order to produce an acting script, the Yankee stage manager, "Mrs. Bateman . . . slashed at it with her bowie knife—and has reduced it to 2 scenes an act, and all the dramatis personae to 7 or 8!" (Martin, *Tennyson,* p. 513). It may have been Irving who shrewdly recognized the timeliness of the play when only five years before the papal see of the Roman church had seen fit to enunciate the doctrine of Papal Infallibility which seemed to many Protestants to make it impossible for Roman Catholics to offer complete national loyalty. James Anthony Froude, Carlyle's house guest and later biographer, crowed: "you will have hit Manning [Roman Catholic Cardinal] & Co. a more fatal blow than a thousand pamphleteers & controversialists" (Martin, p. 513).

Indeed, when Archbishop Cranmer told about promising the "wan boy-king" Edward "if I loved him, not to yield/ His Church of England to the Papal wolf/ And Mary" (Act I Scene ii), there was considerable applause from the audience. But when Mary declaimed "I am English Queen, not Roman Emperor," it was greeted with acclamation, since Victoria had just been named Empress of India!

When Henry James damned the drama as "simply a dramatized chronicle, without an internal structure, taking his material in pieces as history hands them over, and working each one into an independent scene" (Martin, *Tennyson* p. 512), his observation was entirely accurate, but did not take into account the author's intention. This was not to be an *Othello,* but a *Henry IV*; it permitted most of the dim Victorian stage lighting to fall upon Mary, Elizabeth, and Philip, and indeed Mary is portrayed as a figure of great pathos, "never woman meant so well, and fared so ill in this disastrous world" (Act V Scene ii), but the final emphasis was not to be placed on one or more of the three chief protagonists, but upon the epic chronicle of British history. When Tennyson said he was writing an epic history of England in a trilogy of plays, he meant precisely that. Thus the play is composed of twenty-three scenes containing more than forty-three characters. History is full of names and historical incidents and so is Tennyson's play. Full of people and broken into brief episodes, it nevertheless accomplishes exactly what it set out to do. And when James appreciated that it was all done "with rich ability" he was also correct. There are choice lyrical songs and memorable declamatory soliloquies; the pathos of Mary Tudor longing for her Philip's loving return is entirely reminiscent of those waiting women of Shalott and the Moated Grange; the sublimity of Cranmer's recantation of his Recantation is matched by the simple dignity with which Lady Jane Grey met her death on the block; there is peasant humor and country dialect like Tennyson's "Northern Farmer" 1864, sharp cross-questioning like the interior debate of "The Two Voices" 1833, there is the same disgust with the world as "The Leper's Bride" 1889; Mary has the same problem as Arthur—how to make ideals operative in a political world; there is the old problem of obsessive love and obsessive religious zeal as displayed by Lancelot/Guinevere and the Holy Grail; the familiar strain of melancholy is offset by the passages of military and nationalistic fervor; ironic reversal is everywhere present, as when Mary says at the beginning of her reign that no one will be burnt for heresy, and ends up as "bloody Mary," as the champion of the Roman Catholic Church finally breaks its hold on England, as she teaches Elizabeth the hard lesson never to share her throne with a male monarch and never to put her trust in the birth of children. The drama is immensely complex and remarkably variegated. And because it is so seldom read, it seems necessary here to move into a somewhat extended résumé of its content.

Act I, in conventional dramatic manner is essentially Exposition, although it contains many themes and symbols later to be developed. We see Mary and her half-sister (whom she considers illegitimate) riding side by side, the picture of enmity in amity, Mary now triumphant, just as in the last scene, the populace will be hailing Elizabeth as sovereign. Mary welcomes the offer of Charles, Emperor of Spain, of his son Philip in marriage, although the British Privy Council prefers Courtenay, Earl of Devon, the last Plantagenet. From Lambeth Palace Cranmer refuses to flee, and is delivered to the Tower along with Hooper, Ridley and Latimer. At St. Paul's outdoor Cross, Father Bourne proclaims the blessings of the restoration of the Old Faith and Courtenay, popular with the people, has to come to his rescue. He also receives an invitation from Le Sieur de Noailles, the French Ambassador, to attend a meeting of the Wyatt conspiracy. Explaining to Elizabeth that as they are by noble birth both foes to Mary, they should be good friends and perhaps husband and wife, Courtenay is rebuffed by Elizabeth's dogged protest of loyalty to her sister and her designation of him as a "zig-zagging butterfly." Lord Chancellor Stephen Gardiner summons Elizabeth to Mary's presence, suggesting that she withdraw from the Court and seek seclusion at Ashridge in the countryside—which is exactly what the judicious Elizabeth wants. She will stay rigidly free from all associations which could give Mary an excuse to execute, even though she recognizes:

> I am of sovereign nature, that I know
> Not to be quell'd; and I have felt within me
> Stirrings of some great doom when God's just hour
> Peals.

In more friendly fashion, Lord William Howard, Admiral of the Queen's Fleet, sees the danger within her own personality:

> you are one
> Who live that men shall smile upon you, niece.
> They'd smile you into treason.

In Westminster Palace, Mary chats with her lady-in-waiting, Alice, about a miniature of Prince Philip, asking what Henry VIII was like in his youth—"all pure lily and rose / In his youth, and like a lady," is her astonishing reply. Yet Henry, who did not love Mary, gave his love freely to Ann Boleyn, casting off Mary's mother Catherine of Aragon. Cranmer had sanctioned the divorce on grounds that made Mary a bastard. In gossip, Alice quotes Lady Jane Grey as saying that the Communion Wafer is not Christ, but the product of a baker. Mary, eleven years Philip's senior, feels pity for Jane's grace and beauty, wit and youth, and wishes they were hers, although for such a quip about holy things, she may well die on the block. Even Elizabeth, "the bastard sprout," is prettier; everybody is against Philip: Gardiner, the Privy Council, the people, and Parliament. Then follows her impassioned soliloquy:

> But I will have him! My hard father hated me,
> My brother rather hated me than loved;
> My sister cowers and hates me,
> Give me Philip, and we two will lead
> The living waters of the Faith again
> Back thro' their widow'd channel here, and watch
> The parch'd banks rolling incense, as of old,
> To heaven, and kindled with the palms of Christ   (III v)

In a marked recession from her boast of amnesty made to Elizabeth, she affirms

> God hath sent me here
> To take such order with all heretics
> That it shall be, before I die, as tho'
> My father and my brother had not lived.

On the other hand, with unexpected liberality she will pay King Edward's debts, curb the expenditures of her lavish court, and halve the subsidy levelled on the populace.

In a significant colloquy with Lord Chancellor Gardiner, he confesses to the Queen that he goes about in fear for his life because the people so hate the idea of the matrimonial liaison with Spain, and recommends a union with the British favorite, the Earl of Devon (Courtenay). In umbrage, Mary shouts that she is a Tudor and will control her people. But Gardiner presses his argument: Your people will brook neither the Pope nor the Spaniard. Philip is cold, haughty, and has a score of illegitimate sons (and then, *sotto voce*, I have just lost my office by being an honest fool!) With Mary of Scotland married to the French Dauphin, the French Ambassador de Noailles fears that a Spanish marriage will draw England into the war on the side of Spain. Agreeing with Gardiner, he considers Prince Philip to be in every way a lesser man than his father, and one who openly lives a wanton life.

But Simon Renard, Spanish Ambassador, although he bears no letter of formal marriage offer, nor personal letter from Philip to Mary (Mary muses, "Strange in a wooer"), calls Philip "pure as an angel . . . chaste as yourself!" This is what Mary wants to hear, so Renard proceeds with the full agenda: execute Elizabeth or else Philip will not come, bear Philip a son to make Spain's hold secure, let Spanish gold flow freely in bribes to Parliament. When he oversteps by reminding Mary that the Roman emperors did not hesitate to remove impediments to their successful rule, even within the family, Mary regally replies "I am English Queen, not Roman Emperor!" When Renard returns almost immediately with the formal proposal from Philip, Alice sings a scoffing song:

> His friends would praise him, I believed 'em,
> > His foes would blame him, and I scorn'd 'em,
> His friends—as angels I received 'em,
> > His foes—the devil had suborn'd 'em.

Mary returns pale but triumphant from the Council Chamber: "Ay! My Philip is all mine" and sinks, half-fainting into a chair.

Act II opens in Alington Castle, with Sir Thomas Wyatt working to set his father's sonnets in order. But Anthony Knyvett sweeps in, commanding: Tear up that woman's work (father's sonnets), 1,000 Englishmen wait your leadership on Penendon Heath! Sir Thomas objects to such designation of his father's genius:

> Dumb children of my father, that will speak
> When I and thou and all rebellions lie
> Dead bodies without voice. (II i)

He will not stir until he hears from Sir Peter Carew and the Duke of Suffolk; but soon enough (with Victorian drama's immediate response to messages) he receives a cipher from Courtenay that Sir Peter has fled to France and that the Duke will soon to taken into custody. In spite of the bad news, opening the window, he addresses some fifty Kentish men gathered below: First we must save the Queen from her own choice of Philip, second the Spanish Inquisition must not set itself up in England; third, behold what Spanish rule has done to the New World, turning "paradise into hell." At the Guildhall in London, Wyatt demands the safekeeping of Mary, possession of the Tower, and four Council members as hostage. But Sir Thomas White, Lord Mayor of London, raises 30,000 Londoners to protect Mary in "that dim, diluted world of hers" (poor vision) and proceeds to hew the drawbridge into the Thames at Southwark so that Wyatt has to go ten miles out of the way by Kingston Bridge. Although his forces break through to Ludgate, Lord William Howard captures Wyatt and Mary sends Courtenay, Elizabeth, and the dukes of Dudley and Suffolk to the Tower.

The rebellion crushed, the mood of the new times is set by Gardiner who orders that the fresco of Henry VIII at the Gracechurch Conduit have the legend "*Verbum dei*"—the Word of God—painted out and a pair of gloves put in its place—no heresy in gloves! Sir Ralph Bagenhall observes that a hundred rebels in London and hundreds in Kent have been hanged, Lady Jane executed, and Wyatt had exonerated Elizabeth and Courtenay with his last voice: "The tigress had unsheath'd her nails." In the Victory Procession, Mary wore red shoes "as if her feet were wash'd in blood" and Sir Thomas Stafford exclaimed "Why she's grown bloodier!" and Bagenhall observed Mary with Philip:

> She cast on him a vassal smile of love,
> Which Philip with a glance of some distaste,
> Or so methought, return'd.

The papal Legate will give absolution to England for her past Puritan sins and Henry's independency; Philip will make Mary a "wife-widow" by his absences, and England will become a "Spanish province." The Legate is cardinal Reginald Pole, cousin and close youthful friend of the Queen. Amidst her joy in having Pole back from his twenty-year exile, Mary feels a stirring in her womb and rejoices: Philip may be bleak in manner, but her son will clear away all the false Reformation learning of Luther and Zuinglius and end the proud ambitions of Elizabeth. Although Philip acts increasingly like the king of England and the joint Houses of Parliament have voted to acknowledge the primacy of Pope Julius, nevertheless there are stirrings in the opposite direction. Articles have been drawn up that no foreigner may hold office in the royal household, fleet, forts, or army and if Mary dies without issue, the Spanish-English bond will be dissolved. In the meantime, England refuses to support Spain in the war against the French. Reginald Pole may rejoice that "This is the loveliest day that ever smiled on England," and resolve that he has come from Rome to "heal, not harm; not to condemn but reconcile." The past may be forgiven but not forgotten, for when Sir Ralph Bagenhall refuses to kneel to sing the *Te Deum* (having fought valiantly against the papacy under William, Edward, and Henry), he is arrested and taken to the Tower.

When Mary resolves to restore the laws against Lollardism (followers of John Wycliffe), to burn out heresy even if it means the loss of her Crown, a spirited debate breaks out between Gardiner and Pole. When the Cardinal pleads for moderation—"The good Shepherd does not slay the wandering sheep"—Gardiner replies that Pole has himself been tainted by Lutheranism. Stung, Pole reminds Gardiner that he himself acceded to Henry's desire to divorce Catherine, and on grounds which made Mary a bastard. Quite properly, Mary complains that she called the two ecclesiastical gentlemen for counsel and instead got in the middle of a feud. Gardiner reluctantly apologizes, but hands Mary a further list of prominent heretics for burning.

In the meantime, Courtenay has been exiled, and Elizabeth once again rusticated, this time to Woodstock where she writes on a window pane: "Much suspected, of me/ Nothing proven can be" (III v). A fire in her quarters brings her honorable jailor and protector Sir Henry Bedingfield and a milkmaid sings outside about rustic romance and marriage as a contrast to the duels of kings. But rustic romance and marriage are not options for Elizabeth who thinks:

> How oft the falling axe, that never fell,
> Hath shocked me back into the daylight truth
> That it may fall today!

A brusque letter from the Queen summons Elizabeth to Court to wed Prince Philibert of Savoy. She obeys, but with the resolve that when she is "Queen indeed; no foreign prince or priest / Shall fill my throne, myself upon the steps / I think I will not marry anyone."

Arriving in London, she finds the Queen has been in tears for the previous three days because Philip is leaving. But a message from his father to rein in Mary's persecutions and a warning from Renard that "we must not drop the mask before the masquerade is over," convince him to stay one day more, although his father's semi-retirement into cloistral solitude makes him anxious to be about imperial affairs.

In Act IV the burnings, exiles, and imprisonment of heretics goes on apace even when Cardinal Pole, Bishop Thirlby, Lord Paget, and Lord Howard visit to beg that Cranmer be exiled or live a private life, now that he has recanted. Reminding the petitioners that Catholic prelates More and Fisher had both died, Mary laments wryly "My life is not so happy, no such boon,/ That I should spare to take a heretic priest's." When Thirlby reminds her of Cranmer's gentleness, graciousness, and learning, Pole makes an invidious distinction: "These are but natural graces, my good bishop,/ Which in the Catholic garden are as flowers,/ But on the heretic dunghill only weeds" (IV i).

Scenes ii and iii of Act IV have to do with the recantation of that Recantation, and the burning of Cranmer. At first we see him the victim of physical fear, mumbling that "it is against all precedent to burn/ One who recants." Father Bonner, one of his inquisitors, gloats:

> Now you, that would not recognize the Pope,
> And you, that would not own the Real presence, [that Jesus
>   is really present in cup and wafer]
> Have found a real presence in the stake,
> Which frights you back into the ancient faith

Then he is concerned about the length of the burning; will it be brief like Latimer's, but Ridley and Hooper burned for "Three-quarters of an hour." Their faggots were soaked with water to lengthen the suffering; will mine be also? It is a day of rain.

The scene shifts from the Oxford prison to St. Mary's Church where the choir sings the "Nunc Dimittis" ("Let now thy servant depart in peace"), Father Cole malignantly describes Cranmer as downfallen, debased, gone "from councillor to caitiff" and calls upon him to read his Recantation before the congregation. But instead, Cranmer gains the courage to recant his Recantation: My unpardonable sin was to "sin against the light." Then he reaffirms his earlier writings (against the Real Presence in the Sacraments) and confesses the physical fear that drove him to such cowardice:

> For there be writings I have set abroad
> Against the truth I knew within my heart,
> Written for fear of death, to save my life,
> If that might be; the papers by my hand
> Sign'd since my degradation—by this hand
>   (holding out: his right hand)
> Written and sign'd—I here renounce them all;
> And since my hand offended, having written
> Against my heart, my hand shall first be burnt,
> So I may come to the fire.

Then with a parting outburst—at the papacy—"As for the Pope, I count him Antichrist,/ With all, his devil's doctrines, and refuse,/ Reject him, and abhor him." Then as Paget tells us, "He pass'd out smiling." It is also Paget who summarizes all the dizzy shifting of British policy within the period as "Action and reaction/ The miserable see-saw of our child-world,/ Make us despise it at odd hours, my lord."

>   the world is like a drunken man,
> Who cannot move straight to his end, but reels
> Now to the right then as far to the left

And Lord Howard speaks the epitaph:

>   Unhappy land!
> Hard-natured Queen, half-Spanish in herself,
> And grafted on the hard-grain'd stock of Spain—
> Her life, since Philip left her, and she lost
> Her fierce desire of bearing him a child,
> Hath, like a brief and bitter winter's day,
> Gone narrowing down and darkening to the close.
> (Act IV Scene iii)

Lord Howard replies that he has also observed the treatment of heretics of the poorer classes, fed with maggoty bread, chained in breathless dungeon's, drinking putrid water filled with worms, dying of gangrene, cast out naked upon dunghills where they become alive again with maggots so that even a carrion-eating dog would vomit before he tastes. All of this reflects Tennyson's naturalistic description in "Forlorn": "body is foul at best . . . The fairest flesh at last is filth on which the worm will feast . . . This poor rib-grated dungeon of the holy human ghost . . . This Satan-haunted ruin, this little city of sewers. . . ."

The fifth and final act laments the loss of Calais because Mary would not follow the counsel of her military advisors, the dying of Mary, and the succession of Elizabeth. Mary cries out that if her heart were opened, two names would be found there: Calais and Philip, but Sir Nicholas Heath has to inform her that "That gateway to the mainland over which / Our flag hath floated for two hundred years / Is France again." Mary, in an agony of self-examination, calls upon the saints:

> I have rebuilt
> Your shrines, set up your broken images;
> Be comfortable to me. Suffer not
> That my brief reign in England be defamed
> Thro' all her angry chronicles hereafter
> By loss of Calais.

Looking at a broadside posted within the Palace itself, she reads: "Your people hate you as your husband hates you." Thus has her name become a byword:

> Heretic and rebel
> Point at me and make merry. Philip gone!
> And Calais gone! Time that I were gone too!

Then she pronounces what might well become her epitaph:

> Mother of God,
> Thou knowest never woman meant so well
> And fared so ill in this disastrous world.

In a house near London, the Count de Feria sounds out Elizabeth concerning her feelings for Philip in the event of Mary's death, and receives the entirely appropriate reply: "My sister's marriage, and my father's marriages; / Make me full fain to live and die a maid," leaving the Count vowing that he and Philip together will "tame" her independent spirit. Hearing rumors of the Queen's dying, a non-conformist preacher shouts his anarchistic picture of the New Jerusalem out in the street: "break down all kingship and queenship, all priesthood and prelacy . . . cancel and abolish all bonds of human allegiance, all the magistracy, all the nobles, and all the wealthy; and . . . send us again, according to His promise, the one King, the Christ, and all things in common, as in the day of the first church, when Christ Jesus was King."

Sir William Cecil enunciates a doctrine dear to Tennyson and eloquently exemplified in the *Idylls of the King*, that a ruler must have "no passionate faith," but "live by balance and compromise." Then turning to her heir, he considers that this Tudor may be "brave, wary, sane" even if her blood is adulterated by her Boleyn heritage. In a curiously quiet final speech which is nonetheless full of resolve, Elizabeth assesses the future:

> with Cecil's aid
> And others, if our person be secured
> From traitor stabs—we will make England great.

It should be clear from this necessarily cumbersome *résumée* that *Queen Mary* bristles with dramatic incident. Almost every violence is visited upon the characters in the play: exile and death abroad, beheading at the block, immolation by burning at the stake, slow death in prison, torture, rebellion, and the disastrous defense of Calais. Out of the *Dramatis Personae*, Queen Mary dies despairing, the Queen's cousin Cardinal Reginald Pole is summoned to the Inquisition in Rome and dies; Thomas Cranmer, Latimer, Ridley, Hooper are all burned at the stake; Edward Courtenay flees and dies in exile; Sir Thomas Wyatt and his fellow conspirators—Sir Thomas Stafford, Captain Brett, and Anthony Knyvett are hanged, as are a hundred Londoners and hundreds of citizens of Kent. So the play about "Bloody Mary" is very bloody, indeed. However, the rules of Senecan decorum prevail, so that most of the carnage is relayed through messengers rather than agonizing demises in full view of the Victorian audience. Many of the character studies that emerge from troubled times are superb: Cranmer's natural fear of pain over against his loyalty to God's truth; Courtenay, the beautiful butterfly in his zig-zagging flight, Lord William Howard's unswerving patriotism, the suave and elegant scruples of Cardinal Pole, the marvelous courage of Sir Thomas Wyatt steadfastly going to a battle already lost (like the Pendragon in the Last Grey Battle in the West), the sliminess of Simon Renard and the Count de Feria, the brutality of the churchmen Bonner and Cole, the insightful singing of the ladies-in-waiting to Elizabeth and the Queen. But without question the central drama is played out between Mary, Philip, and Elizabeth.

Poor misguided and misunderstood Mary—so loyal to the great things in her life, so deprived of love from her own father and brother and finally deprived of her mother. In the realm of love she never faltered: Catherine of Aragon, the Catholic Church, her unloving consort, and her hoped-for child never born. Even in her patriotism, she may well have thought, as several times she said, England was a small island nation which would gain immeasurably from becoming part of the great Spanish Empire which ruled most of the Old World (except for France) and all the known New World. Deficient in eyesight; compared with Elizabeth uneducated, plain and old before her time, and because of her twin loyalties to Philip and Catholicism, a figure which otherwise would have been pathetic, forced to became monstrously and inhumanly villainous. From the brilliance of the accession to the throne in the first scene, we are compelled, by an unpleasant attention, to watch everything she valued slip away, every decision mistaken, every relationship compromised, until we recognize that long before she died in her bed she was personally dead. This is a painful and yet compelling figure.

Philip is a far less engrossing figure. His allegiance to the Catholic Church is minor by comparison with his dominant desire to advance Spain, please his father, and rule every situation in which he finds himself. Indeed, toward the end, even his doting Mary asks if it is right for him to be fighting against the Pope in Italy: "the Pope is now colleagued with France;/ You make your wars upon him down in Italy—/Philip, can that be well?" To which Philip replies with terse contempt: "Content you, madam;/ You must abide my judgment, and my father's."

On the other hand, Tennyson seems to say first that Philip, too is a victim along with his hapless wife, forced to marry a woman, plain, losing her sight, ungainly, and eleven years his senior, as a human hostage to Spain's grandeur. On two occasions, amidst her own immense self-pity, Mary acknowledges that he too has been victimized. But Tennyson's major defense is to show that Philip is a practitioner of *realpolitik*; he recognizes in the sixteenth century what was not generally glimpsed until our own time, that every concept, relationship, or value is in some manner political. So religion, marriage vows, public promises and private threats are all ultimately negotiable for political advantage. He had reason to be haughty; it was his Machiavellian grasp of how power operates in the real world that made him cold. He took innumerable mistresses and sired many illegitimate children with no personal involvement because he is essentially the walking, talking Presence of the Spanish Empire, a symbol rather than a man. And is it not possible that in the naive innocence and simplicity of loyalties that composed Mary, what she really fell in love with were his pride, his presence, and his symbolism? But when Renard urges him to be kinder to his wife and he accedes, it is never because he felt a single stirring of sympathy, it was only that at the moment, kindness was the right currency to use to purchase the ultimate political advantage. This, Mary could neither understand nor accept, and so she earned more contempt from her husband-antagonist who knew the rules of the game and how to keep the score, whereas she still thought she was playing a simple hand of Romance/Marriage/Motherhood, quite forgetting that the rules are entirely different for queens, unless she wanted to be a pawn.

Elizabeth Tennyson was stuck with. There was no place in this drama for the gay dancing girl or for the aging but powerful queen. All he had to work with was the waiting-game, but this was different from Marianna of the Moated Grange. She waited hopelessly and finally longed for death; Elizabeth waited, with talons hooded, ready for the acceptable moment when she could suddenly reveal who she was. Skillful in dialogue, easily able to out-maneuver most of the male characters, her main characteristic is steely self-control and this is not very useful on the stage. She sees in her future two alternatives: the Axe and the Throne. The invitation to the first would be a tactical error in her policy of loyal non-alignment; the invitation to the second would be by the pall-draped door of her half-sister's death. But along the way, we see her learning several useful lessons: no lovers, no husband, no children, and always the steering of a sane and sensible middle course even when her Tudor-Boleyn blood boiled.

So in a play with many tragical elements, the Mary story is essentially pathos, ending with the pathetic wail: wanting to do so well, how did I end up doing so ill?

Queen Guinevere

The most detailed and psychological study of Queen Guinevere of Cameliard is found in the eleventh book of the *Idylls of the King*, "Guinevere" 1859. Lancelot has brought her to the convent at Almesbury and departed to his own country. The King, assuming that Guinevere was with his former friend, laid siege to his castle, which gave Modred, with the backing of the heathen kings of the North, the opportunity he had awaited to wrest the Kingdom from his lord (much like Tostig in *Harold*).

Her identity unknown to the holy sisterhood, the Queen's gentle stateliness so charmed them that they willingly gave her shelter from her enemies and assigned a little waiting maid to do her bidding. Like the serving ladies-in-waiting of *Queen Mary*, this adulterous queen has her heart searched and torn by the gay prattlings and songs of innocence. The most particularly unnerving one was based on the Parable of the Wise and Foolish Virgins (Matthew 25) from which Tennyson distilled the sorrowing chorus:

> Late, late so late! and dark the night and chill!
> Late, late so late! but we can enter still.
> Too late, too late! ye cannot enter now.

It was Modred who spied upon the Queen and her lover, and having been told by Vivien that they will meet and then part forever, quickly brings his henchmen and cries "Traitor, come out, ye are trapt at last," only to be hurl'd headlong by Lancelot and borne fainting away by his men. But Guinevere recognizes that she will "be for evermore a name of scorn."

Although Guinevere resolves "Not even in inmost thought to think again/ The sins that made the past so pleasant" nevertheless "from old habit of the mind/ [her thoughts] Went slipping back upon the golden days." The central issue of her preference for Lancelot pivots around the definition of Arthur's manhood. The *envoi* "To the Queen," defines the King as "Ideal manhood closed in real men," but the little novice in Almesbury adds that her father called him "more than man." When Guinevere first met Arthur, she "thought him cold,/ High, self-contain'd, and passionless"—a bit like Mary's first glimpse of Philip. And she hugged to herself the warm reflection: "Not like my Lancelot." It was a bard to the novice's father who put the whole relationship in mythic fashion:

> could he find
> A women in her womanhood as great
> As he was in his manhood, then, he sang
> The twain together well might change the world.

It is interesting to observe that just as Mary needed Philip—"I must have him"—just so Tennyson had earlier contended that in order for Arthur to do his great work in the world he must find a woman as great in her womanhood as Arthur in his manhood and then (and then only?) "The twain together well might change the world"—which was, of course, Tennyson's intention for Arthur.

The final Pre-Raphaelite scene, with her "milk-white arms and shadowy hair" outlined against the stony convent floor, leads Arthur to say some insufferably self-righteous things. "Well is it that no child is born of thee"—and we are reminded of that later poor Queen who longed above all else to bear a child and heir to Philip. Then Arthur drives in the blade further: "The children born of thee are sword and fire,/ Red ruin, and the breaking up of laws." When he announces "I march to meet my doom,/ Thou hast not made my life so sweet to me,/ That I the King should greatly care to live" it is almost an exact match to Mary's wry reply to those who begged for the freedom of Cranmer: "My life is not so happy, no such boon,/ That I should spare to take a heretic priest's." Arthur moves from bathetic self-pity: "I, whose vast pity almost makes me die" to a stunning assumption of God-like prerogative: "Lo, I forgive thee, as Eternal God / Forgives!" Then in a downward swoop he claims "I was ever virgin save for thee," and that he was never a "smaller soul, / Nor Lancelot, nor another."

Guinevere makes a final assessment which fits with her earlier criticism of the problems of being married to a God-like husband.

> my false voluptuous pride, that took
> Full easily all impressions from below,
> Would not look up, or half-despised the height
> To which I would not or I could not climb—
> I thought I could not breathe in that fine air,
> That pure severity of perfect light—
> In Lancelot I yearn'd for warmth and color which I found

Echoing the prophecy of the bard, she cries out:

> Ah my God,
> What might I not have made of thy fair world,
> Had I but loved thy highest creature here?

And then, in a frequent Tennyson *Coda*, she chides herself that passion ought always to be in subservience to duty:

> It was my duty to have loved the highest;
> It surely was my profit had I known;
> It would have been my pleasure had I seen,
> We needs must love the highest when we see it,
> Not Lancelot, nor another.

Realistically, like "Bloody Mary," she knows what false impression she has left for history:

> The days will grow to weeks, the weeks to months,
> The months will add themselves and make the years,
> The years will roll into the centuries,
> And mine will ever be a name of scorn

Also, like Queen Mary, her final reliance is on the glories of Heaven:

> That in mine own heart I can live down sin
> And be his mate hereafter in the heavens
> Before high God!

Whereas Queen Mary died, with husband *in absentia*, Guinevere, with husband in the Far Country, will work out her salvation in a litany of good works:

> and so wear out in alms-deed and in prayer
> The sombre close of that voluptuous day
> Which wrought the ruin of my lord the King.

Both heroines had erred in the realm of excess: Mary with an excessive domestic love untempered by her patriotic duties as Queen and Guinevere with the voluptuous excess that finds passion outside domesticity and is lured away from the highest duties by the flickering phantoms of "warmth and color."

Queen Victoria

"To the Queen," written in March, 1851 and prefixed to the first Laureate Edition of Tennyson's poems, included a stanza on the Crystal-Palace, omitted in subsequent editions. In the very first quatrain, Tennyson introduces a significant comparison. Whereas the previous monarchs of England were ranked according to military prowess—"the warrior kings of old"—Victoria's reign will be seen as "nobler" than them all. Surely the Laureate recognized that he was making an invidious gender distinction, this time in favor of the feminine monarch above the masculine.

Gracefully he alludes to his royal appointment as Poet Laureate to succeed William Wordsworth by referring to his laurels as greener coming from the brows "Of him that uttered nothing base." A quatrain establishes the "wild March" season, then the sixth quatrain moves to the issue that was so important to Queen Mary: "leave us rulers of your blood," a pious hope abundantly fulfilled by Victoria's nine children. Thus in this thirty-six line toast, we see Tennyson pulling together many of the tensions which tore earlier and later poems: Victoria loved her husband, yet was also a good mother to their children; she was married to a foreign aristocrat, but was able to enlist his aid in her own patriotic efforts; she had high ideals, yet was more able than King Arthur to make them effective in the real world; she was sincerely religious, yet never considered a withdrawal from daily duties like Emperor Charles of Spain (*Queen Mary*); she managed to pull a whole era, not just her own country, into the orbit of her personal moral concerns, so that "Victorianism" always had a moral flavor.

Of course the "Dedication" to the *Idylls of the King* is addressed particularly to Prince Albert, Queen Victoria's consort, nevertheless, the portrait of the husband is integrally related to the character of the wife. The first quartet of the *Idylls*; published July 1859, contained "Enid," "Vivien," "Elaine," "Guinevere," as they were then entitled. Amidst the warmest public admiration, Prince Albert sent a note asking for the poet's personal inscription: "You would thus add a peculiar interest to the book containing those beautiful songs, from the perusal of which I derived the greatest enjoyment. They quite rekindle the feeling with which the legends of King Arthur must have inspired the chivalry of old, whilst the graceful form in which they are presented blends those feelings with the softer tone of our present age" (W.J. Rolfe, *The Poems of Tennyson*, p. 302). After the Consort's death in 1861, when the Queen went into a period of deep mourning for more than three years, wearing "widows weeds" for the remainder of her life, Tennyson's tribute was particularly appropriate and adroit. Albert "held them dear," and so they could become a literary memorial. Then the poet dares to establish a supposititious kinship "perchance as finding there unconsciously / Some image of himself" and this will be the major emphasis of the dedication.

Tennyson saw Albert as King Arthur's "ideal knight," conscientious, working to redress human wrongs, too high of spirit to speak or entertain slander, and then, most gratefully to the Queen: "Who loved one only and who clave to her." Now that he is gone, we can finally estimate his contribution to the life of the nation, most modest, self-effacing, disciplined, not lured by "wing'd ambition," nor seduced by the opportunities for pleasure, but throughout

> Wearing the white flower of a blameless life,
> Before a thousand peering littlenesses
> In that fierce light which beats upon a throne

The "noble Father of her [England's] Kings to be," he labored for the poor and pointed forward to a day in which the terrible waste of war will be replaced by the "fruitful strifes and rivalries of peace," an "ampler day" filled by literature, science and art.

***

Then, turning to Albert's widow (how often he referred to himself as Hallam's "widow" in *In Memoriam*!) he adjures her not to indulge in heart-break, but remembering the closeness of their comradeship during the years of marriage, let her endure as royalty and wear her Crown in "lonely splendor."

The last stanza is in the familiar form of a Victorian benediction: May his love still "o'ershadow" her, may the love of their sons "encompass" her, may the love of their daughters "cherish" her, may the love of her people "comfort" her—all in the sure knowledge that in some glad Heaven, God's love will set her once again at her husband's side.

The *envoi* "to the Queen" at the close of the *Idylls* is even more closely reasoned and rich in topical reference than the "Dedication." Somewhat awkwardly he reminds Victoria that even when Albert was extremely ill, he attended the public thanksgiving on February 1872, for the recovery of the Prince of Wales from typhoid fever.

Pale as yet and fever-worn, the Prince
Who scarce had pluck'd his flickering life again
From halfway down the shadow of the grave.

The cablegrams of congratulation for his recovery coming from many parts of the Empire Tennyson called "thunderless lightnings striking under sea."

When Manitoba was added to Canada in 1869, Scottish merchants protested the cost of maintaining the American possessions—thus anticipating the modern colonialism in which the dominant country does not take possession of the colonial lands, with all the attendant expenses of education, defense, hospitals, and missionaries, but simply maintains a two-way procession of raw materials to England and manufactured items from England, without the expense of social and military programs. Tennyson castigates the money-minded merchants and asks if they would prefer a "Forever-broadening England" or "a sinking land,/ Some third-rate isle half-lost among her seas?" Returning to his "Dedication" to Prince Albert, Tennyson asks the Queen to accept the *Idylls* because of her continuing devotion to Albert to whom he had dedicated the first four idylls. Avoiding the problems implicit in the early manuscripts of Geoffrey of Monmouth's *Historia Regum Britanniae* and Sir Thomas Malory's *Morte d'Arthur*, he presents the "old imperfect tale" in a new perspective of "Sense at war with Soul; / Ideal manhood closed in real man." In a time pointing toward international conflict, he deplores those who "loose" the national religion, whose energy has been sapped by the prosperous years of peace, cowardly souls who care only for gold, the groans of labor, the "poisonous honey stolen from France" (a Galliphobia Tennyson exhibited in "Locksley Hall Sixty Years After"). God's goals for the world lie beyond sight, but if Englishmen maintain their common sense, then fears of the future will be only "morning shadows huger than the shapes / That cast them," and not as in the *Idylls of the King* "The darkness of that battle in the west / Where all of high and holy dies away."

***

Tennyson's social criticism of the shopkeeping mentality is clear and strong. He is a royalist, an imperialist, and a loyal supporter of his imperial sovereign. And after having shown in twelve books how even a semi-divine king was unable to hold together a savage and divided realm, he seems to be saying to Victoria—but you can do better!

"On the Jubilee of Queen Victoria," was written in commemoration of the fiftieth anniversary of the Queen's accession, 1887 and printed in *Macmillan's Magazine* for April. William Gladstone was one of Tennyson's large readership who resented the sour note struck by the volume of December 1886, *Locksley Hall Sixty Years After Etc.* For half a century he had fought hard for social and economic progress and now the laureate, made a lord of the realm by his recommendation, seemed to be denying that there had been any progress. So he wrote an article for the *Nineteenth Century* listing all the reforms achieved since 1842 and reminding the poet that "Justice does not require, nay rather she forbids, that the Jubilee of the Queen be marred by tragic notes."

Perhaps the Laureate agreed with Gladstone's position, because it is quite different from his other poems dedicated to the Queen, even in format: eleven cantos, alternating between three lines of unrhymed trochaic pentameter and eight-line stanzas of unrhymed trochaic pentameter, each stanza ending with the word "Jubilee." The bard celebrates her "kindliness" rarely found among monarchs; a queen and the Empress of India, her reign has been long and the crown never "worn by the worthier." Never the lawless despot, never vulgar, nor vainglorious, always gracious, gentle, great and queenly. He invites all Britons to light their mountain beacons tonight and deck their houses for the Jubilee. Victoria, woman and queen, was true to both callings and because she always sorrowed "with the sorrows of the lowest," then let her Jubilee be a great time of sharing with the lowly and the destitute, the maintenance of hospitals and food for the needy.

Henry's fifty years of reign are "all in shadow," Edward's fifty years "gray with distance," and her Grandsire' fifty years "half forgotten." So let some patriotic architect raise a stately memorial to tell the centuries how great was the reign of Victoria!—a time of Commerce, Science, Empire. Let the residents of Albion, from aristocrat through manufacturer to laborer join with the populace of Canada, India, Australia, and Africa to sing praise of this golden Jubilee year.

Then in the only negative images, the poet seems to hear "thunders moaning in the distance . . . spectres moving in the darkness." But in a quick return to the positive, he assures his readers that the "Hand of Light" will be Victor over spectre, darkness and thunder, and "Dawn into the Jubilee of the Ages."

Chapter V

ℰℭ

Dane, Saxon, and Norman: *Harold*

L aying claim that "This trilogy of plays portrays the making of England," the poet categorized the first of the epic trilogy (although not in order of composition): "In Harold we have the great conflict between Danes, Saxons, and Normans for supremacy, the awakening of the English people and clergy from the slumber into which they had fallen, and the forecast of the greatness of out composite race" (*Memoir* II 173).

Having learned many painful lessons through the publication and stage presentation of *Queen Mary*, Tennyson, eagerness unabated, forged confidently ahead to write another historical drama, only half the length of the previous play and using a vocabulary strong and spare, adopting a masculine point of view (rather than the starring role of stage tragediennes characteristic of *Queen Mary*), but the drama had to wait half a century for staging!

Of this same enormously active period in his poetic productivity, Prof. Hughes observes that "In the spate of dramatic monologues written concurrently or succeeding the dramas, we find greater compression and more effective interplay of speaker and auditor" as Tennyson "honed" his craft (*The Manyfacèd Glass*, p. 195). As the *Idylls of the King* had raised the question: Can the Ideal ever be realized in the arena of political expediency? and *Queen Mary* had poignantly dealt with the related question: Can love, marriage and an heir save a realm? so this first play of the historical trilogy asks an even more pointed and humanistic question: Can a man maintain his integrity and be a king?

Aubrey de Vere responded to *Harold's* "Aeschylean strength . . . epic spirit combined with dramatic form," fulfilling the Laureate's high hope for the trilogy both as an epic and the history of the making of England. Since Bulwer-Lytton had written *Harold. Last of the Saxon Kings*, it seemed appropriate to dedicate *Harold* to his son, the Right Honorable Lord Lytton, Viceroy and Governor-General of India. He acknowledges that the Bayeux tapestry and the Roman de Rou, Edward Freeman's history of the Norman Conquest and Bulwer-Lytton's "historical romance treating of the same times, have been mainly helpful to me in writing this drama. Your father dedicated his 'Harold' to my father's brother; allow me to dedicate my 'Harold' to yourself." The dedication was particularly gracious and wound-healing because of Bulwer-Lytton's published comments on "O Darling Room" in *The New Timon*; "school-miss Alfred" "out-babying Wordsworth and out-glittering Keats" and the more general Bulwer critique of the 1845 addition to the pension-list: the "Theban taste" that "pensions Tennyson while starves a Knowles."

In preparation for the settings of *Harold*, Tennyson had taken his son Hallam to the site of the Battle of Senlac Hill and there had written the Petrarchan sonnet which became the epigraph of the drama, "Show-day at Battle Abbey 1876." Starting in a garden (familiar Tennysonian site), he quickly hears "The cuckoo yonder from an English elm / Crying, 'With my false egg I overwhelm / The native nest,'" thus making quite clear his basic preference for the Saxon over the Norman. He fancies he hears the ring of harness and battleaxes on Norman helms; he sees the dragon-banner of the realm (like the banner of Arthur the Pendragon). Did Might make Right in the battle eight centuries before? Perhaps historically military power "makes for good," but on the individual plane, the two protagonists, Saxon Harold and Norman William, must finally vindicate their deeds before the Judgment of Heaven.

The criticism has often been made that Carlyle, Arnold, Rossetti, Swinburne, and Tennyson somehow sanitized and idealized their portraits of the medieval era. But Henry Wadsworth Longfellow, in America, thought the tone and voices exactly appropriate to the middle ages: "I have just been reading your 'Harold' and am delighted with its freshness, strength and beauty. Like 'Boadicea,' it is a voice out of the past, sonorous, strange, semi-barbaric. What old ancestor of yours is it thus speaking through you? . . . The Fifth Act is a masterly piece of dramatic writing. I know not where to look for anything better" (December 21, 1876; Lang, Shannon eds. *Tennyson Letters*). To this encomium, the often painfully honest or brusque Laureate replied: "I have had many congratulatory ones [letters] about *Harold*, but scarce any that I shall prize like yours. You ask 'What old ancestor spoke through you?' I fear none of mine fought for England on the Hill of Senlac, for, as far as I know, I am part Dane, part Norman" (Lang & Shannon, II). Although Mary Gladstone considered *Harold* "superior to Queen Mary in every respect" (Lang & Shannon 135), she could scarcely forget the two and one half hour reading of it by the playwright from eleven to one-thirty in the afternoon, by which time lunch had spoiled and the domestic staff departed to other tasks, and Papa, [the Prime Minister of England] had simply become "sleepy, not forthcoming."

In some ways *Harold* travels the same roads as *Queen Mary*. In both dramas the historical situation is made complex by the shadowy presence of a ruler whose attention has turned from this world to the spiritual world to come. Philip of Spain is so powerful and vindictive in his political machinations because his father, the Emperor, has slipped away into the conventual life of penance and meditation; so Harold, not of the royal line, is always hampered by the previous commitments and the present inertness of Edward the Confessor. Promises have been made which shape all the military action: Edward's promise to William of Normandy that he should become his heir, the promise of Harold to his father that he would never turn England over to the Normans, the deceptive promise of Harold that he will support William's ambitions (in order to rescue his brother Wulfnoth from the Norman dungeons), the promise of Edward that his ward Edith should never marry but go into lifelong religious retirement, and the promise of Tostig that his brother would never rule England. A kind of stately and tragic dance steps in and around these life-giving or life-taking pledges. The ultimate tragedy of the historical drama is that in the spurious world of politics, promises, as originally meant and taken, cannot be fulfilled with the original integrity of purpose.

Professor Hughes points out the strong accent on "legitimacy" in both dramas. To Mary, Elizabeth is the Boleyn bastard; to Cranmer,

Mary is the "Spanish bastard" because Leviticus states that a man ought not to marry his brother's wife. Thus there is a tendency among the British populace to prefer Courtenay because there is no question but that he is the last Plantagenet. In *Harold* there is some question about Harold's sonship to Godwin or to a peasant stable hand, and William of Normandy is often referred to as "the French bastard." The play is firmly textured within dreams and visions. For example, when Edward receives a vision of death at Sanguelac—the Lake of Blood, we know that it will come to pass. However, despite these ruling foci of the play, essentially just as in *Queen Mary*, it will be stuffed to bursting with English history and historical characters like any chronicle. It is the first episode of the "making of England" and so characters will be seen in their public rather that their private faces, although several main characters emerge as studies of personality. The dilemma of Harold who seeks to maintain his personal integrity in an unideal world is powerful and dramatic. William the Conqueror has at least dual personalities. Edith doesn't fare very well, but her foil Aldwyth is courageous, cunning, and deeply in love. Tostig, the man of unsettled passionate mind creates his own hell out of lack of sane moderation, just as Queen Mary was excessive in religious zeal, Queen Guinevere in sexual longing, and the quest of the Holy Grail in excessive devotion to otherworldly ideals.

The first act focuses upon a terrifying comet presaging war, or punishment for the mistreatment of Norman clergy, depending on the point of view of the speaker. The passionate Tostig, who cannot even rule himself, is determined to succeed Edward on the throne, but Edward, grateful for Harold's twelve years of military and governmental service which had made his life of prayer and meditation possible, announces: "Thou art the man to rule her [England]!" Tostig admits that his brother is "wise in peace and great in war" and thus ought to be king. Nevertheless, his passionate nature makes him demand a kingship even he knows he is ill-prepared for.

When Harold tries to warn Tostig of incipient rebellion in his earldom of Northumbria, Tostig vows to crush it by any means. Harold mildly applies horsemanship: "if they prance,/Rein in, not lash them, lest they rear and run." Loefwin jestingly describes Tostig as a man who cannot smell a rose without pricking his nose. Harold explains that since the King and Queen have always spoiled him, "Now the spoilt child sways both." Weary of his many tasks during the previous decade, Harold requests a brief vacation to hunt and hawk beyond the seas. Edward agrees, but with ordinary prescience tells him to go nowhere near Normandy. Edith also begs Harold to stay. Aldwyth, listening in the thicket, vows she could love Harold ten times more than this fearful child and in soliloquy bares her ambition to be Queen of England. Planning to urge the compliant Edward to send Edith to a nunnery during Harold's absence, she knows how to trick Harold into marrying her in order to win the support of the Saxon barons: "Peace-lover is our Harold for the sake / Of England's wholeness."

The second act exactly plays out the dire forebodings of King Edward and Edith. The scene opens on the beach at Ponthieu; it is night and Harold's ship had been lured onto the rocks with torches carried by the local fishermen, who thus amplify their meager income: "ye fish for men with your falsefires"—an ironic variant on Jesus' invitation to the fishers on the banks of the Sea of Galilee that if they will follow him, he will make them "fishers of men." While they engage their royal catch with peasant humor, a messenger summons Count Guy of Ponthieu to capture Harold for "rot or ransom." Guy would have employed the rack for a huge ransom, but William of Normandy has other plans. Recalling how heroic Harold had been in leading the Normans to victory for William over Brittany, he offers him full release if he will promise to support his claim to the throne of England. Two pressures work heavily upon Harold to make him resign his own claim to the throne. His brother Wulfnoth has long been imprisoned by William and pleads pitifully to be set free— "for my sake, O brother!" In addition, Edward the Confessor had foolishly promised the throne to William and the Normans.

Upon this second act the hand of fate lies heavily. William muses "fate . . . hunted him," and complacently sermonizes: "God and the sea have given thee to our hands." The heroic Harold is willing to face the savage punishments William levies upon prisoners who thwart his will. His brother's sufferings move him, but "Not even for thy sake, brother, would I lie." Even His love for Edith cannot stir him, but his vow to his father that he would never permit the Normans to rule England breaks his resolve. For his filial promise and for the sake of England, he, the invariably truthful, will lie, and so he consents to support William's claim before the Witan—having "lost myself to save myself."

Shamefacedly he confesses to his brother; "I mean to be a liar," and Wulfnoth, aware what this resolve is doing to Harold's integrity as a man of honor and the heir to the throne, sadly replies: "Forgive me, brother, I will live here and die." But with Norman craftiness, William makes Harold swear not simply before him and his nobles, but before the "holiest shrine in Normandy." William sweetens the bitter pill by promising to unite "Anglo, Jute, / Dane, Saxon, Norman."

In the third act, we see the dissolution of everything that was hopeful at the beginning of the drama. As Edward lies dying, Archbishop Stigand judges the king as one who had "conscience for his own soul, not his realm." Tostig curses Harold and flees England to mount an invasion from abroad. Harold's sister hates him because he is the cause of Tostig's banishment. Wulfnoth remains a hostage in Normandy despite Harold's lying vow. Harold and Edith cannot wed because Aldwyth had persuaded the king that Edith should be a perpetual cloistered virgin as penance for the king's foolish vow to Norman William and for Harold's deceitful vow sealed upon relics of the holiest saints of France.

The Archbishop, having made all his treasure at Ely available to Harold's cause, also absolves him from his false vow, but on a deeper level, ponders "Is naked truth actable in true life?" In other words, is personal integrity possible in a private life, and is absolute truth possible in the political realm? From the vision of Nebuchadnezzar, Tennyson borrows Edward's apocalyptic dream: "I saw, and beheld a tree in the midst of the earth . . . and the height reached unto heaven . . . in it was meat for all: the beasts of the field had shadow under it, and the fowls of the heaven dwelt in the boughs thereof . . . and behold a watcher and a holy one came down from heaven. He cried aloud, and said thus, Hew down the tree . . . Nevertheless, leave the stump . . . in the earth'" (Daniel 4). Unshaken by the Biblical vision, Edward persists in his naming of Harold to the throne and cannot comprehend all the fuss about Edith: " . . . a wife, / What matters who, so she be serviceable / In all obedience?"

Edith laments, "crown'd King — and lost to me!" then sings a lovers' lament much like the folk ballads of Scotland and Ireland. But Harold counsels her, "sell not thou / Our living passion for a dead man's dream." For the militant Harold, the Norse battle gods sometimes seem superior to the saints at peace, particularly those upon whom he swore to cede the throne to William. He will need gods of battle because Tostig has gathered the kings of Norway, Scotland, Ireland, Iceland, and Orkney for an invasion. William has exposed the false oath to Pope Hildebrand, who proclaims that "all Christendom is raised against thee [Harold]," and gives England to William.

But the massing of foes does not dismay Harold who notes the irony: "The Lord was god and came as man — the Pope / Is man and comes as God." Act IV traces the fortunes of war at the Battle of Stamford-Bridge, in which Harold holds back "The hugest wave from Norseland ever." Having gained the Danes to fight against the invasion by promising to wed Aldwyth, he laments the death of "our dear, dead traitor-brother Tostig," and his thanes, deep in their cups, sing praises to the Norse Thor:

> Mark'd how the war-axe swang,
> Heard how the war-horn sang,
> Mark'd how the spear-head sprang,
> Heard how the shield-wall rang,
> Iron on iron clang,
> Anvil on hammer bang —

But upon news that William has landed at Pevensey with 1,000 ships, 100,000 men, thousands of horses, he turns in anger upon the revellers: "The curse of England! these are drown'd in wassail / And cannot see the world but thro' their wines!" (cf. Tennyson's heavy dependence upon port wine).

The final act fulfills the prophecy of Edward the Confessor that Harold would die on Senlac ("Sanguelac") Hill. The hero, like Arthur in *Idylls of the King*, goes forth bravely to a battle which is already lost, and lays down his life for the sake of England: Am I "the last English king of England?" he asks, and Edith, become prophetess, replies: "No, / First of a line . . . coming from the people, / And chosen by the people." At Stamford-Bridge he had loved the Norse king for his honor as a king and integrity as a man, but this William —"I hate / This liar who made me liar."

He and William ride out to battle on the day of their birth, with three Normans to every Englishman, Norman William kills Gurth, Harold's loyal henchman, and Harold is slain by Norman arrows.

The Conqueror muses that Harold was killed by three things: St. Peter (the Papacy), the betrayal of the Northumbrian earls after he had wed Aldwyth to win their fealty, and a chance arrow sharpened by the Norman saints upon whom Harold had sworn a false oath, and resolves to build a church on the site of Harold's death.

Turning to Aldwyth, he promises to treat her with honor for Harold's sake, but she moans the complaint of Cain after he slew his own brother, "My punishment is more than I can bear." The play ends with the reiterated pledge of William the Conqueror: I will "Make them again one people — Norman, English / And English, Normans; we should have a hand

> To grasp the world with, and a foot to stamp it —
> Flat. praise the Saints! It is over, No more blood!
> I am King of England. . . ."

Edward Bulwer Lytton,
Harold, The Last of the Saxon Kings

Since Alfred Tennyson freely admitted, in the dedication of Harold to Lord Lytton, that "the Bayeux tapestry and the Roman de Rou, Edward Freeman's History of the Norman Conquest, and your father's Historical Romance treating of the same times, have been mainly helpful to me in writing this Drama," surely a comparison of the drama to the novel is appropriate.

The immediate and most striking contrast between *Harold* and *Harold, the Last of the Saxon Kings* is generic. The two-volume novel has space and time to expatiate on event and characterization that are denied to the three-hour stage presentation. For example, an entire chapter (I, iii) of the novel can be devoted to the assembling of the Witana-gemot in the great hall of Westminster, whereas, in the spare drama the very first scene of the first act already accepts the sons of Godwin as exiles returned and amalgamated into the loyal populace. Thus the historical novel tends to assemble a vast cast of characters along with many interlaced subplots and histories.

Indeed, a related contrast is stylistic: the compendious lyric poet writes in spare, masculine language, whereas the historical novelist employs all the lush verbiage of poetry. At the close of his novel, Bulwer Lytton spreads a canvas full of capitalized generalities:

> Eight centuries have rolled away, and where is the Norman now? or where is not the Saxon? The little urn that sufficed for the mighty lord [William the Conqueror] is despoiled of his very dust; but the

tombless shade of the kingly freeman [Harold] still guards the coasts, and rests upon the seas. In many a noiseless field, with Thoughts for Armies, your relics, O Saxon Heroes, have won back the victory from the bones of the Norman saints [upon which Harold vowed to support William's claim to the English throne]; and whenever, with fairer fates, Freedom opposes Force and Justice, redeeming the old defeat, smites down the armed Frauds that would consecrate the wrong, — smile, O soul of our Saxon Harold, smile, appeased, on the Saxon's land!

By comparison, the playwright is content for his peroration with the covert threat:

> "Praise the Saints! It is over. No more blood!
> I am King of England, so they thwart me not,
> And I will rule according to their laws."

Of course the novel is free to expand on Hilda the Morthwyrtha, the altar of Thor, Druid runes and Wicca rites at a length simply not available to the drama. Surprisingly, both novel and drama employ the use of interspersed songs — not unexpected for a lyric poet, but more rare for a novelist. The dream vision is also prevalent in both genres, perhaps as memorial to such great dream visions of medieval prose and poetry as *The Pearl* and *The Vision of Piers Plowman*. These visions contribute both to Bulwer Lytton and Tennyson the grand sense that the history of England was ultimately in the hands of the Fates, rather than the presumptuous decisions of petty men. Rather like the inevitability of the Gospel of Matthew, the future had been foretold by prophets (Isaiah, Ezekiel, etc.) eight centuries before, so that while the scripts lay waiting for 800 years, all history waited for was the arrival of the actors to speak the words and perform the plot. Harold, tricked by Norman William into making a vow upon the bones of the Christian saints, is also trapped by the sure expectation of division from his beloved Edith (too close in kinship to be permitted by the Church) and a random arrow falling out of the heavens as revenge of the Norman relics for broken vows. Even the location of Harold's last battle is delineated by a Norman name which, translated into English, means "lake of blood."

Although Tennyson shares Bulwer Lytton's historical determinism, they have rather different estimates of the character of William the Conqueror. He appears in the novel as a ducal leader skillfully fulfilling his destiny to join the Normans and the Saxons. But in the drama, Tennyson, no doubt infected by the Victorian love of melodrama, tends to shape him as a stage villain to be hissed for his manipulative love of Edward the Confessor, breaking his promise for the release of his hostages, and tricking the last Saxon king into a vow bound not simply by feudal custom but by the sacrosanct bones of the saints.

Indeed Tennyson is still engrossed in raising a consideration he earlier delineated in *Queen Mary*: Everything I did was for the good of England and the honor of the Holy Catholic Church — and all of it went wrong! "never woman meant so well,/ And fared so ill in this disastrous world." Harold is a man of such perfect integrity that all, friend and foe alike, respect and trust him. But the questions remain: is personal integrity enough and can it operate in a kingdom's politics which are always dominated by public compromise of many points of view rather than the particular integrity of one man and his individual point of view.

Tennyson had explored this private/public tension before in earlier major poetic works. Did "Ulysses" have the social right, after only three years' return from the Trojan War to decide "I cannot rest from travel," in order to assuage his absenteeism from his city-state Ithaca, by turning his kingly responsibilities over to Telemachus" by slow prudence to make mild/ A rugged people, and thro' soft degrees/ Subdue them to the useful and the good." Surely the restless monarch ought to have "subdued" his own travel-lust and given Telemachus his turn to explore "that untravell'd world."

Even the quest for the Holy Grail could become a lure to political irresponsibility.

> "I said
> To those who went upon the Holy Quest,
> That most of them would follow wandering fires,
> Lost in the quagmire? — lost to me and gone,
> And left me gazing at a barren board,
> . . . . . leaving human wrongs to right themselves."
>
> ("The Holy Grail," lines 883-94)

The mad-woman of "The Palace of Art," having given her life to the collection of *objets d'art*, finally seeks a mere cottage in the vale . . . "Where I may mourn and pray." The Lady of Shalott was an industrious creative artist until Sir Lancelot went tinkling by. The web disintegrated, the mirror cracked, the loom went idle, and the boat ride to Camelot became an exquisite suicide technique.

"The Lotos-Eaters" is perhaps the strongest exhibit for evasion of social obligation. Not only do the mutinous mariners abandon ship, they also renege on nationality, patriotism, marriage vows, parental responsibilities. In their total surrender to the sedative seduction of the lotos, they blunt the Victorian edge of colonialism and affront Victorian religious sensibilities by their delineation of the gods as "careless of mankind," lying stupified "beside their nectar," smiling "in secret" at the catalogue of human woes: "wasted lands," "Blight and famine, plagues and earthquake," wars, "flaming towns, and sinking ships." When the gods evade their duties, what can be expected of Odysseus' navy? The glory of the jilted protagonist of "Locksley Hall," is that he disgustedly puts aside his South Pacific fantasy in favor of engaged participation in a world with airplanes overhead and an eventual "Parliament of man, the Federation of the world" ahead.

Of course it is Thomas Carlyle who provided the Gospel of Work to the Victorian era. As late as Joseph Conrad's *Heart of Darkness*, 1902, Marlow is saved from the degradation of Kurtz by his fidelity to duty. The Bible of *Heart of Darkness* is Towson's manual on seamanship. Marlow asks and answers his own atavistic question:

"You wonder I didn't go ashore for a howl and a dance? Well, no — I didn't. Fine sentiments, you say? Fine sentiments be hanged! I had no time. I had to mess about with white lead and strips of woolen blanket helping to put bandages on those leaky steam pipes — I tell you. I had to watch the steering and circumvent those snags, and get the tin-pot [decrepit Congo river steamer] along by hook or by crook. There was surface truth enough in these things to save a wiser man."

Saved — by fidelity and technology!

In his preface, Edward Bulwer Lytton did his best to differentiate between the novels of Sir Walter Scott, the research of historical scholarship, and his own composition of Historical Romance. "The great author of *Ivanhoe*, and those amongst whom, abroad and at home, his mantle was divided, had employed History to aid Romance; I contented myself with the humbler task to employ Romance in the aid of History" (I, xiv). Claiming to have consulted all the original documents "as if intending to write, not a fiction but a history," as novelist he stressed event and characterization. It was "that inward life" of men and women "which becomes the fair domain of the poet."

So when the real Poet Laureate pared down the sprawling canvas of Bulwer Lytton's Historical Romance, we catch a glimpse of the playwright's genius. Tighter in format, with more intense focus on fewer, but more central characters, Tennyson has crafted the historical novel into the taut pattern of Aristotle's "tragic hero." First he introduces the audience to the character that all men admire. By compromises that disgust him most of all, he reaches the dreamed of apex of political power. In his predestined fall from that high place, we are encouraged to admire mankind because of his personal integrity and his hope for the eventual union of Dane, Norman, and Saxon in England.

Duke William summed up the mysterious forces that brought him down—not only fatal flaw, but the will of the gods:

> "a warrior,
> And wise, yea truthful, till that blighted vow
> Which God avenged today . . .
>
>   "holy Peter fought for us,
> . . . the false Northumbrian held aloof,
> . . . that chance arrow which the saints,
> Sharpen'd and sent against him" (V, ii)

Thus Tennyson's Harold, last of the Saxon kings, was foretold by dreams and visions, but slain by a Pope, offended saints, and a chance Norman arrow.

Chapter VI

෨෬

They Murdered the Archbishop in His Own Cathedral: Tennyson, *Becket*; Eliot, *Murder in the Cathedral*; and Anouilh, *Becket*, or *The Honour of God*

Queen Mary, that vast historical chronicle, had received polite accolades from reviewers and only median support from theatregoers. *Harold* (cf. Bulwer-Lytton, *Harold, Last of the Saxon Kings*), despite its comparative brevity (half the length of *Queen Mary*), did not stir Henry Irving to produce it at the *Lyceum*, perhaps because it contained no starring role for him, and, although published in November 1876, it did not receive dramatic production for half a century. In point of publication, it came four years later than "Gareth and Lynette" and "The Last Tournament," immediately followed *Queen Mary* in 1875 and preceded "Montenegro" (1877), "The Revenge" (1878), and *The Lover's Tale* (1879).

Despite the hurly-burly of Lionel's wedding to Eleanor Locker at Westminster Abbey and the disappointment of *Harold* being so ignored, Tennyson set about valiantly writing *Becket*, a complex subject requiring considerable historical research. By 1879 the first proofs were run off, but the play was not officially published until December 1884. Once again an abortive dance was joined with Irving. Apparently Irving admired the drama but was aghast at the formidable financial risk involved in its production. Prof. Martin refers to his troubled cogitation: "with an outlay of two thousand pounds upon the production," £135 expenses per night, income only £150 nightly at best, including no fee for the playwright, "you may calculate the position of the manager at the end of a run of one hundred nights" (523). *Mary* had lasted only 23 nights and *Harold* had not yet been presented to a not very eager public.

Irving had refused the play in 1879; but asked leave to produce it in 1891. In the meantime Tennyson had decided to set it aside and work on Irving's uncertain invitation: "a less remarkable work . . . would have a greater chance of success" (Martin 523). Privately Irving assured a friend (Wilfred Ward): "Tennyson is a great poet, but he cannot write plays; what a pity he tries, they are the greatest rubbish!" But facing the Poet Laureate at Aldworth publically, he made a series of obeisances and abjectly inquired "You don't disdain to be ranked with Shakespeare?" When the remark was repeated, loudly, to the increasingly hard-of-hearing Tennyson, displeased, he grumbled "I think he must be chaffing me" (Maisie Ward, 174). Ironically, just before Tennyson' death, deciding for some esoteric reason that the times were now ripe for the play, he produced *Becket* in 1899, when it became one of his greatest acting roles with Ellen Terry as Rosamund.

The disappointment entailed in the delays of production was echoed in the dedication to the Earl of Selborne: "to you, the honoured Chancellor of our own day, I dedicate this dramatic memorial of your great predecessor; — which, although not intended in its present form to meet the exigencies of our modern theatre, has nevertheless — for so you have assured me — won your approbation." Perhaps Tennyson was ruefully recalling the tremendous incisions made by Mrs. Bateman in his *Queen Mary* manuscript. *Becket* was nearly as long as the original uncut *Mary* and considerably longer than Shakespeare's *Hamlet*, with a cast of well over forty, an elaborate exposition in the form of a Prologue, plus five full acts, containing fourteen scenes and multiple changes of setting.

Tennyson's major purpose in the plays was to show "the awakening of the English people and clergy from the slumber into which they had for the most part fallen, and the forecast of the greatness of our composite race [Danes, Saxons, Normans]. In 'Becket' the struggle is between the

Crown and the Church for predominance, a struggle which continued for many centuries" (*Memoir* II 176-185). With the addition of *Queen Mary*, Tennyson sets himself to describe "the dawning of a new race," he, so much more gifted in the description of dissolution and decay, the mourning dove changing its tone to simulate the lark ascending! The major difficulty in proving that "after the era of priestly domination comes the era of the freedom of the individual" lies in the comparative rating of protagonists of the two historical dramas.   Queen Mary is an ultimately pathetic rather than tragic figure, displaying "the final downfall of Roman Catholicism in England" by default, not by any positive act. Becket (one of Irving's great stage portrayals) would persuade the audience of the splendor of the Church and the moral penury and corruption of the Crown. So that, based on the strength of the protagonists, both Church (Mary) and Crown (Henry II) emerge scarred and inadequate, with, if anything, the preponderance of moral power on the side of the Church!

The mood of the Prologue is the last idyllic portrayal in the drama. Becket is Henry's "true lover and friend" (line 40), to whom the King can safely leave the care and protection of his beloved mistress Rosamund de Clifford when he departs for Anjou or Normandy. But there are two Serpents in this Garden. Eleanor of Aquitaine is a strong and remorseless villainess in this *Becket*. A French troubadour, with greater intellectual powers than her perpetually boyish husband, she cares nothing for his female playthings but fears the existence of Rosamund because she is true wife in terms of affection and the mother of Henry's beloved son. Eleanor stands in the line of the great French troubadours, mother of Marie de Champagne, compiler of the chivalric code of aristocratic "courtly love." She muses:

> Louis of France loved me, and I dreamed that I loved Louis of France; and I loved Henry of England, and Henry of England dreamed that he loved me; but the marriage-garland withers even with the putting on, the bright link rusts with the breath of the first after-marriage kiss, the harvest moon is the ripening of the harvest, and the honey-moon is the gall of Love; he dies of his honey-moon. I could pity this poor world myself, that it is no better ordered. (208-219)

The other Serpent is Henry's misconception of Becket's loyalty — completely given, but with the codicil that it cannot exceed his sense of personal integrity.

As part of the idyllic friendship between the son of the Earl of Anjou and the "Cheapside brat," the King, over the objections of his friend, makes the Chancellor of the Exchequer also Archbishop of Canterbury "a man of this world and the next." With the cool prescience that marks his every thought, Becket foreshadows the whole tragic chronicle by musing, right at the play's beginning: "God's favor and king's favor might so clash / That thou and I —" (156).

When Herbert of Bosham announces the death of the old Archbishop, Henry can only pass it off with "Well, well, old men must die, or the world would grow mouldy, would only breed the past again" — an unfeeling version of the deeply-felt words of the dying King Arthur to Bedivere:

> The old order changeth, yielding place to new,
> And God fulfills himself in many ways,
> Lest one good custom should corrupt the world. (Morte
> d'Arthur," 1835)

And when Herbert relays the Archbishop's recommendation that Becket be his successor, the king is ecstatic — "Thou hast but to hold out thy hand." But both Edens are poisoned: the Eden of manly loving loyalty and the pastoral Bower where Rosamund awaits her lover.

Exposition having been provided by the Prologue, the first act immediately shows Rosamund rescued from Fitzurse and de Tracy by Becket. Emerging from passionate soliloquy, Becket returns the great seal of England.

> O thou Great Seal of England,
> Given me by my dear friend, the King of England —
> We long have wrought together, thou and I —
> Now must I send thee as a common friend
> To tell the King, my friend, I am against him.
> We are friends no more; he will say that, not I.
> The worldly bond between us is dissolved,
> Not yet the love. Can I be under him
> As Chancellor? as Archbishop over him?
> Go therefore like a friend slighted by one
> That hath climb'd up to nobler company.
> Not slighted — all but moan'd for. Thou must go.
> I have not dishonor'd thee — I trust I have not —
>   [Tennysonian dubiety]

Not mangled justice. May the hand that next
Inherits thee be but as true to thee
As mine hath been? 0, my dear friend, the King!
                              (I, i. 183-198)

The king, like the later Henry VIII, considers the old Archbishop's death a time to enforce the royal will upon both nobles and the church. So he sends a series of demands, which he calls "customs:" both laity and clergy will be subject to the King's Court, the revenue of vacant bishoprics shall revert to the Crown, the successors shall be approved by King and Council, clergy may not leave England by sea without King's permission. Becket, moved by the warning of Bishop Roger of York — "Wilt thou destroy the church in fighting for it?" — signs the demands but does not affix the Great Seal. So the King rages and agonizes to Fitzurse:

And Becket had my bosom on all this;
If ever man by bonds of gratefulness —
I raised him from the puddle of the gutter,
I made him porcelain from the clay of the city —
Thought that I knew him, err'd thro' love of him,
Hoped, were he chosen archbishop, Church and crown,
Two sisters gliding in an equal dance,
Two rivers gently flowing side by side —
But no!

My comrade, boon companion, my co-reveller,
The master of his master, the King's king —
God's eyes! I had meant to make him all but king.
Chancellor-Archbishop, he might well have sway'd
All England under Henry, the young King,
When I was hence. What did the traitor say?
False to himself, but ten-fold false to me!
The will of God — why, then it is my will —
Is he coming? (I, iii, 252-275)

Tennyson's most characteristic criticism of Becket and Henry is that they always turn toward extremes rather than the middle way, a *via medias*, later chosen by the Anglican Church as the midway point between Rome and Geneva. Gilbert Foliot, Bishop of London, becomes the playwright's spokesman:

As Chancellor thou wast against the Church.
Now as archbishop goest against the King;
For, like a fool, thou know'st no middle way.
                                    (I, iii, 104-106)

Appeals to the Roman Pontiff will not save Becket; because the Pope at Rome most of all desires Henry's help against the Pope at Avignon and the Emperor. So the Act ends with the London crowd crying "Blessed is he that cometh in the name of the Lord" — a clear reference to Christ's Palm Sunday entrance into Jerusalem, but at its fringes the sobering question, could the Jerusalem crowd protect Jesus from his attackers? The fourth scene evokes yet another Christologic echo, when the archbishop has his servants shepherd the poor of the London street to dine on the banquet prepared for earls and barons (Luke 14:16-24). Singing "Black Sheep, White Sheep," the beggars, with the threat of plague-infection shield the archbishop from the four knights vowed to his assassination.

Just as the first act ended with a beggars' chorus, the second act begins in Rosamund's Bower with a duet "Is it the Wind of the Dawn?" Rosamund, amid pastoral surroundings urges the king to be friends again with Becket and challenges his royalty lest, like Herod the Great's massacre of the Innocents (Matthew 2:16), he had sent all Becket's kin — babes, orphans, mothers, into exile in France. The king reflects that Eleanor's hatred of Becket is a natural class animosity, but his is "A bastard hate born of a former love."

At a meeting in Montmirail, King Louis of France, former husband of Eleanor, seeks to arbitrate between Henry of England and the self-exiled Becket. The twin watchwords that disrupt the arbitration are both Becket's: "Saving mine honour, " and "Saving God's honour," and Becket ruefully agrees with Foliot of London: "I am too like the King here; both of us / Too headlong for our office," once again sounding Tennyson's central insistence upon a preferable middle way.

The third act will once again begin with song, "Babble in Bower" by Margery, new maid to Rosamund in the Bower. In a long, folksy monologue (48 lines), she retails gossip and her royal assignment. Unbelievably Rosamund seems not to know about the annulment of Eleanor's marriage to the "monk-king" Louis, followed by her wedding with Henry, or of the plan for the crowning of young Henry (Eleanor's son) as future successor to his father, by the bishops of York and London.

Finally stirred to interdict, the Pope excommunicates all England. Suffering under this heavy judgment, Henry makes peace again with Becket:

> Give me thy hand. My Lords of France and England,
> My friend of Canterbury and myself
> Are now once more at perfect amity. (III, iii, 177)

but significantly, they do not exchange the kiss of peace.

The Serpent boldly enters Rosamund's Eden in Act IV, as Eleanor catches little Geoffrey (Henry and Rosamund's son), is sent into a rage by the sight of the elaborate jeweled Cross she gave Henry about Rosamund's throat and, dagger in hand, attempts to force Rosamund to admit she is not married to Henry and her son a bastard. In one of those declamatory scenes beloved by the Victorians, Rosamund dares to reply:

> Both of us will die,
> And I will fly with my sweet boy to heaven,
> And shriek to all the saints among the stars:
> "Eleanor of Aquitaine, Eleanor of England
> Murder'd by that adulteress Eleanor,
> Whose doings are a horror to the east,
> A hissing in the west!" Have we not heard
> Raymond of Poitou, thine own uncle — nay,
> Geoffrey Plantagenet, thine own husband's father—
> Nay, even the accursed heathen Saladeen —
> Strike!
> I challenge thee to meet me before God. (IV, ii, 137ff.).

Equally beloved to Victorian and contemporary melodrama, Becket appears to the rescue. Fitzurse is dismissed with a curse, Eleanor claims it was all a farce, and Rosamund is dispatched for safety to the nunnery at Godstow. Fearlessly, Eleanor boasts bravely that to rid himself of her would lose Henry her great duchy of Aquitaine, foolishly that the king would not dare to imprison her (*The Lion in Winter*, cinema).

Act V opens in a castle in Normandy with Henry accusing Eleanor of urging the just-crowned Henry III to raise a rebellion against his father. But the magnificently-eloquent Queen stings him with the fact: "The brideless Becket is thy king and mine!" Reminding him that she brought him to his throne by commissioning thirty-six ships with the riches of

Aquitaine, and that she has borne him four brave sons. Displaying her trump card, the Cross she had given him, she accuses him of keeping Rosamund as paramour, and then taunts:

>   King Thomas, lord
> Not only of your vassals but amours
> Thro' chastest honor of the Decalogue
> Hath used the full authority of his Church
> To put her into Godstow nunnery. (V, i, 109-113)

And in the pangs of doubly-thwarted love, Henry cries out "Will no man free me from this pestilent priest?"

Using an argument picked up by both T.S. Eliot and Jean Anouilh, John of Salisbury admonishes Becket: "He loses half the meed of martyrdom / Who will be martyr when he might escape." Then the four knights, vowed to rid their king of "this pestilent priest," convey Henry's demands to Canterbury: lift the ban of excommunication and do not seek to make Henry III's coronation void. Quite sincerely the archbishop claims to have loved the Prince only second to his father. Before the full spiritual authority of the archbishop in his own cathedral, the knights rush out, pell-mell, but John does not hesitate to rebuke his spiritual lord with the full force of common sense. "Is strength less strong when hand-in-hand with grace: (*Sauvitur in modo, fortiter in re*) and then puts the situation into a terse epigram: "They seek — you make — occasion for your death."

The bell rings for Vespers. Taking up his great Cross, he intones "I go to meet my King!" Quoting from the second Psalm of the Old Testament and the fourth chapter of the Acts of the Apostles from the New Testament, Becket moves to stately music to conduct Vespers in the North Transept of Canterbury Cathedral. The monks flood into the Chancel from the Cloister. Becket, alone in the transept, demands the great doors of the Cathedral be opened, quoting from the Sermon on the Mount: "Knock and it shall be open'd." He presents himself to the knights with the words from the Gospel of John: "I am he whom ye seek" which Christ uttered to the Temple police come to arrest him in the Garden of Olives. Just as he spoke to Grim and John, I cannot bear a hand on my person, so he brushes off Fitzurse, "Touch me not, for I am not yet ascended unto the Father" (John 20:17, often referred to as *noli me tangere*). No wonder De Brito replies "how the good priest gods himself! / He is not yet ascended to the Father." While Rosamund pleads for mercy, Fitzurse strikes off the Archbishop's mitre, wounds his forehead, and De Tracy's sword falls on Grim's arm and wounds Becket, who falls on his knees: "At the right band of power — / Power and great glory — for the Church, O Lord — / Into thy hands, O Lord," quoting from Christ's seventh word from the Cross (Luke 23:46), he sinks prone. It is De Brito who delivers the final, killing blow: "This last to rid thee of a world of brawls!" Stunned, now that the deed is done, Fitzurse gapes "What! the great archbishop!" and De Morville pronounces their own epitaph: "Will the earth gape and swallow us?"

Crying "King's men, King's men" they rush out of a Cathedral illuminated by lightning while Rosamund, a 13th century *mater dolorosa*, kneels by the martyr's body.

T.S. Eliot, *Murder in the Cathedral*, Written (in abbreviated form) for the Canterbury Festival, June 1935

There are obvious and subtle similarities between Tennyson's *Becket* and Eliot's *Murder in the Cathedral*. The most obvious is the semi-equivalence of Tennyson's lyric melancholy and Eliot's incantatory tone (as if intoned liturgically by an ecclesiastic). The very nature of incantation is the weaving of spells which involve magic repetition and not sudden, dramatic outbursts. This tone is most telling in Eliot's choruses of the Women of Canterbury and the priests of the Cathedral — a Classical device Tennyson does not use. Nevertheless the Tennyson emphasis on mourning for what is lost and his tendency to subsume tragedy into regret effectively silences both the high notes of hilarity and the low notes of barbaric emotion, leaving only a middle, singing range very much like Eliot's priestly incantation.

Contributing to this basic similarity is the Tennyson preference for the via medias of common sense and the Eliot tendency to match any extremity by its opposite: "living and partly living," the priests' counsel: do not fight an intractable tide, and the women's lament that God is slipping out of Canterbury. Eliot's Interlude (Thomas à Becket's Christmas Sermon, 1170) repeatedly makes the point of matching opposites to create a wry realism: Power is present/ Holiness is hereafter; Christ's Birth on Christmas / His Death in the Christmas Mass; mourning / rejoicing; Christ's peace / the World's peace.

Tennyson tends to mute the drama of assassination by clear delineation of the two chief characters (Henry II, Becket) so that we are left with a personal inevitability rather than a shocking event. Eliot, in the chorus of priests, mutes the particular terror of Becket's death by immersing it in the historical echoes of other martyrdoms: St. Stephen, John the Apostle, and the Holy Innocents of Bethlehem massacred by Herod the Great. In a way, both poets tend to displace "sordid particulars" in favor of "eternal design" — for Tennyson the implacable polarity of personalities; for Eliot the outside-of-time foreknowledge of the divine order. As Tennyson has Becket give only conditional loyalty to Henry — "Saving my honour; saving God's honour," so Eliot phrases it "Saving my order, I am at his [Henry's] command." Eliot's Thomas is accused of replacing gratitude by anathema. Both poets mention the unforced exile of the Archbishop retaliated by the enforced exile of his family and adherents by the King; and Eliot's Becket quips: "I am not in danger; only near to death," all events proceed "to a joyful consummation." Tennyson's Becket, dying, "commends" his soul to God; Eliot's more institutional concern "commends" the Church to God. Eliot's wonderfully wry summation through the lips of Richard Brito — "he decided upon martyrdom," therefore the verdict is "suicide while of unsound mind;" exactly matches Tennyson's oft-repeated warning that to choose martyrdom as a means of eternal power and glory is somehow spiritually fraudulent. Both poets rejoice in a historical catastrophe which is redeemed by giving Canterbury "another saint and martyr."

Tennyson, in chronicle fashion, wants to tell us everything about Becket; Eliot, more wisely, picks up the tale only from the return out of the seven-year exile up to the martyrdom. Eliot does not surprise us with his many Biblical echoes; Tennyson does by actually quoting Scripture even more than the rather clerical Eliot. The later poet dares to reproduce a Christmas sermon in its entirety; Tennyson, with all the back-log of Victorian church and chapel going, does not. Tennyson's knights have little adequate excuse (we are King's men and tipsy, too); whereas Eliot has them make a fully-reasoned defense before the tribunal of history much like the epilogue of G.B. Shaw's *St. Joan*. But for both playwrights, there is a wry observation of the very historical crime coupled with some dimension of the ideal and spiritual meaning of history.

Jean Anouilh, *Becket, or the Honour of God*, 1961

Anouilh's *Becket* is a different matter entirely. Whereas Tennyson portrayed Henry II as a spoiled juvenile who never grew up, and Eliot as the secular force which is always arrayed against the divine Plan, Anouilh makes him a homosexual lover suffering the pangs of unreciprocated love! His portrayal of Eleanor is equally unhistorical. For Eliot, Eleanor is largely absent from *Murder in the Cathedral*. For Tennyson, she is the heiress of the Aquitaine troubadours, the foundress of the chivalric code of Courtly Love, and the prime source of powerful, unrelenting evil in *Becket*. But for Anouilh she becomes a flat-faced bourgeois princess pettishly and weakly retelling her domestic woes! Surely the French writer knew better and simply skewed her historic character in order to focus more exclusively upon the love/hate relationship of Henry/Becket.

In the form of a four-act flashback, Henry begins the play kneeling at the martyr's tomb and plaintively asking: Well Thomas, are you finally satisfied? I kneel naked at your tomb waiting for your monks to come and flog me!

The love-affair proceeds with Henry confessing that he never had an idea in his head that Thomas had not put there [But history shows Henry II to have been a powerful and effective monarch]. He now kneels in Becket's Cathedral because, loathing Saxons, he yet needs their help to ward off his sons' grab for the throne.

Clearly pivotal for Anouilh is the opening scene of the protagonists naked together, Thomas rubbing down Henry after his bath. The two youths spar amorously together, Henry calling Thomas "my little Saxon," Thomas bashfully confessing he loves intimate acts of helpfulness with his lover-king, Henry reciprocating in the confessional by mumbling "I scare easily."

So, as in many modern homoerotic affairs, there is one member who loves money, worships power, and is avant garde: Becket's father became rich by "collaborating with the Normans," he adores luxury, "I have a new set of gold dishes," and "two forks." So Thomas tries to instruct the powerful, eternally boyish king in the use of the fork. An effete intellectual consorting with a playful young barbarian. When Henry observes that Thomas is "thinking all the time," he playfully tosses him the Triple Lion Seal and makes him Chancellor of the realm.

Anouilh likes to describe Thomas as " . . . pirouetting . . . graceful as a young boy." In a Saxon hut, espying a filthy Saxon girl hiding in the hay, the King is immediately aroused to heterosexual ardor. But when Thomas protects both her and Henry, sulking, he protests "Do you love me, Becket?" Thomas replies that in releasing the peasant he is protecting the King "Because I love you." When Henry demands Thomas sing his lament for his dear mother (a Saracen), he observes that for the cultured one, morality is simply elegant esthetics (Scene vi). Thomas confirms the observation by sending Gwendolyn, his mistress who truly loves him, to the King's bed, meanwhile musing that just as his Saxon father became rich by collaborating with the Norman conquerors, so "there is a gap in me where honour ought to be" — a reading diametrically opposed to Tennyson and Eliot's insistence that Becket cares consistently for his own honor and the honor of God. In return for Gwendolyn, Henry sends Thomas the Saxon peasant girl, but, when she tries to kill the King, he creeps terrified into Becket's bed, waking from a dreadful nightmare, fantasizing how much simpler the relationship would be if both were either Saxon or Norman, quite unconscious that it is the class and national difference that makes the attraction powerful.

After a notable victory on the Continent, Henry wishes to reward Thomas with the archbishopric of Canterbury, but Becket immediately foresees that the strain between loyalty to Crown and Church will destroy their old, loving fellowship. When he resigns the chancellorship, the childish Henry whines: "you've sent me back the three lions of England, like a little boy who doesn't want to play with me anymore . . . I am alone! Oh, my Thomas, only I loved you and you didn't love me" (III, i).

Confronted by a snivelling Queen, Henry proudly affirms "he gave me with open hands, everything that is at all good in me," then, brutally "I don't like my children . . . your body was an empty desert, Madam — which duty forced me to wander in alone. And Becket was my friend, red-blooded, generous, and full of strength" (III, iii). The amatory tone returns when in the midst of a political confrontation with Becket, Henry blurts out "Did you ever love me?" In Scene iii Henry's mother lays the whole situation on the table: "It is England you must think of, not your hatred — or disappointed love — for that man . . . neither healthy nor manly." Even while Henry begs his barons ("faithful hounds") "will no one rid me of him," he sobs hysterically "I believe I still do [love Becket]."

A peal of bells announces victory and the Saxon mob link Henry and Thomas' names as responsible for victory over the poor little prince Henry in the rebellion instigated by his mother.

So far as Tennyson's *Becket* is concerned, it is important to remember that at the very same time, in a great rush of energy, he was also writing a philosophical poem as dialectic of hope versus despair — "The Ancient Sage;" a vision of world history — "Vastness;" no less than seven Lincolnshire dialect monologues — humorous, subtle, realistic, utterly unsentimental; two poems on the tragic despair of the lower classes — "Rizpah" and "Despair;" and three celebrations of historical feats of heroism — "The Revenge," "Defense of Lucknow," and "The Charge of the Heavy Brigade at Balaclava." In this incredible spate of poetic energy, *Becket* emerged as, in many aspects, his finest production for the stage.

Chapter VII

ଛୀରେ

A Domestic Idyll: *The Promise of May*

"A surface man of theories, true to none"

The "domestic idyll" genre becomes apparent as early as the *Dramatis Personae*. One single member of the county gentry, Mr. Philip Edgar and the middle-class schoolmaster, Mr. Wilson, are submerged in a sea of farmers, laborers and servants. The setting is unapologetically rural, a farmhouse providing background. All Tennyson's former historical dramas had featured the lives of royalty and the fate of nations. Even his short, popular plays: *The Falcon* centered about two aristocratic Italian houses, *The Cup* returned to the exploits of kings and the outreach of the Roman Empire. This *The Promise of May* bears a relationship to his previous plays similar to the dialect folk poems like *Enoch Arden*, "The Northern Cobbler," "The Village Wife," "Northern Farmer, Old Style" in comparison with Tennyson's more elegant examination of Classical (Augustan) themes and the Arthurian legends (Medieval Romantic). As he tended to humanize aristocracy, he also endowed ordinary folk with high heroism and the possibilities of tragedy.

Beginning with an eightieth birthday celebrated by "haäfe th' parish," with dinner in the long barn, the play quickly introduces the two female protagonists, the Misses Dora and Eva, and then proceeds to the principal antagonist Squire Edgar. Dora sings an appropriate Cumberland ditty, concluding with the cheerful chorus "O, joy for the promise of May" and the doleful refrain "O, grief for the promise of May," setting up Tennyson's usual tension between opposites, with much commuting backward and forward, but no final resolution of antinomies (Smith, *The Two Voices*). Dora continues the tension in her comment to Dobson: "the day's bright like a friend, but the wind east like an enemy." Dobson is the heavy-accented farmer who loves Miss Eva but suspects she is more interested in Squire Edgar. But he waxes prophetic about the Squire:

> What's a hartist? I doänt believe he's iver a 'eart under his waistcoat. And I tell ye what, Miss Dora: he's no respect for the Queen, or the parson, or the justice o' peace, or owt. I ha' heard 'im a-gawin' on 'ud make your 'air — God bless it! — stan' on end. And wuss nor that, when theer wure a meeting o' farmers at Little Chester t'other daäy, and they was all a-crying out at the bad times, he cooms up, and he calls out among our oän men, "The land belongs to the people."

So Dobson is the good-hearted rustic swain, at the very beginning critical of Master Edgar. Loving the "owd ways," he hates the books that call them into question, the schoolmaster Wilson because he teaches them, and Edgar because he approaches reading a book. The book proves man to be "an automatic series of sensation," suggesting the philosophies of John Locke and William Godwin, and representing to Edgar the sensational theories that lay behind the altruistic self-interest of John Stuart Mill and Utilitarianism—the enemy of all natural affection in Dicken's *Hard Times*, and making Edgar resolve he is "here! to crop the flower and pass." Whereupon Tennyson slips up and calls "Let us eat and drink, for tomorrow we die" an "old Scripture text"! Meanwhile Edgar muses "if my pleasure breed another's pain, / Well — is not that the course of Nature too . . .?"

Farmer Steer, father to Dora and Eva, congratulates himself on his progress from a laborer to an eighty-year-old landlord who sees to it that his daughters are reared to be ladies. Now he limps from pursuit of someone who forced the passage window by Eva's chamber (Eva turns red and then white). But the footmark in the flower bed must have been made by a "Lunnun boot."

Meeting Edgar, Dobson suspiciously asks to measure his London boot, but, refused, departs muttering "I promised one of the Misses I wouldn't meddle. " Edgar is left to cogitate that if Dobson is sweet on Eva, that attachment might provide marriage and legitimize her pregnancy, leaving him free of any entanglement. After all marriage is only an outmoded tradition and he has already paid for one such transgression. Having gotten the daughter of one of his father's tenants pregnant, he was ruthlessly displaced as heir by his younger brother, leaving him to support himself by pen and brush. Also marriage to even a prosperous farmer's daughter would lead his haughty Uncle Harold to disinherit him.

Edgar muses that in the coming political revolution, thrones, churches, rank, traditions, customs, marriage will all be swept away. Matrimonial partners, desiring other mates, will simply "Bid their old bond farewell, with smiles . . . [and] good wishes. " Once the belief in an after-life is stripped away, man can be seen like the animal kingdom, "A beast of prey in the dark" (cf. *In Memoriam* "Locksley Hall," "Locksley Hall Sixty Years After"). Conventional Vice in Edgar's day may be considered Virtue in the coming age of freedom (cf. "Morte d'Arthur").

When Eva interrupts his soliloquy, he gives her a lecture on Evolution:

> And when the man,
> The child of evolution, flings aside
> His swaddling-bands, the morals of the tribe,
> He, following his own instincts as his God,
> Will enter on the larger, golden age,
> No pleasure then tabood; for when the tide
> Of full democracy has overwhelm'd
> This Old World, from that flood will rise the New,
> Like the Love-goddess, with no bridal veil,
> Ring, trinket of the Church, but naked Nature
> In all her liveliness.

Small wonder that Eva replies, "What are you saying?" and that the Marquis of Queensberry should leap to protest this definition of freethinking atheism!

When Edgar gallantly breaks off a branch of apple blossoms for Eva, she responds like the daughter of an apple-grower: "how wasteful of the blossom you are! / One, two, three, four, five, six — you have robb'd poor father / Of ten good apples. " He, like the typical philanderer, manufactures business in London, but says they will always be friends. Unladylike or not, Eva is bright enough to argue with his choice of words: "friends" should be replaced by "lovers" and the "married parents of her coming child." Indeterminate as always, Edgar weakens and asks her to flee with him, then mentions marriage in the parish church, and finally a license to marry which he will obtain in London — with no intention of doing so. He stifles any sense of personal responsibility by the male formula: "she that gave herself to me so easily / Will yield herself as easily to another."

Five years pass between Acts I and II. Dobson now, still mourning for the exile from home of the disgraced Eva, brings flowers to Dora as proposal for her hand. Dora has been overwhelmed by the absence of her beloved younger sister, the ill success of the farm with mounting debts, her father's breakdown and blindness, and besides, she has hated all men since receiving the letter from Eva: "I have lost myself, and am lost forever to you and my poor father. I thought Mr. Edgar the best of men, and he has proved himself the worst. Seek not for me or you may find me at the bottom of the river. — Eva." With conventional rustic morality, Dobson moralizes: "Thy fayther eddicated his darters to marry gentle foälk, and see what's coomed on it." Quite sensibly, Dora asks how well she would "take to the milking of your cows, the fatting of your calves, the making of your butter, and the managing of your poultry?" To Dobson's credit, this was not at all what he had in mind; he envisioned a genteel wife who would sit in the parlor and play the piano. He would even learn to curb his occasional habit of drinking overmuch. But Dora proudly dismisses him, and his haymakers jolt by on the wagons singing "The Last Loäd Hoäm" about two haymakers in love, working side by side, swearing

> to be true
> To be true to each other, let 'appen what maäy
> Till the end of the daäy,
> And the last loäd hoäm.

So, as in his historic trilogy, the simple rustics often exhibit faithfulness unknown to their aristocratic "betters." But good things still come to betrayer gentry. Philip Edgar has now inherited his uncle's estate and has taken their family name in acknowledgment. As Mr. Harold, he has returned to claim his inheritance, but still remembers Eva's sweetness with regret. But his human reactions of shame and sorrow are stifled by the mechanistic formula "if man be only / A willy-nilly current of sensations — / Reaction needs must follow revel."

Remorse then is simply a part of that "Reaction" by which lying Nature tries to make the Heir of Destiny feel guilty for Her faults. His own grandfather had experienced difficulties with women in his day and now he is "haunted by / The ghosts of the dead passions of dead men," quite confounding that "poor philosopher" Locke with his claim that the child is a "*tabula rasa*," without distinguishing family inheritance. Instead each child bears in "invisible ink" the low drives of our Darwinian ancestry: "Lust, Prodigality, Covetousness, Craft, / Cowardice, Murder."

When Harold and Dora meet on a bridge, he thinks her to be Eva and tells Dora that the foul betrayer is dead in Somerset, passing off his father's death as his own. Dora recalls the stormy morning when they found Eva's bed empty, a desolate note suggesting death by drowning, her father's immediate attack of paralysis, subsequent blindness, and loss of interest in his formerly beloved farm. Harold begs leave to visit the blind father, kissing her hand in a manner she compares favorably with Farmer Dobson's. The tête-a-tête on the bridge is shattered by news that one of her farm hands, Dan Smith, has accidentally run over a lady in the Hollow, so Harold and Dora hasten to the house, and it slowly dawns upon Dobson that this gentleman is no other than the villain Edgar.

Actually the villain has thought of doing "Courtesy to Custom," even he in the vanguard of a new age, to repair the ill to Eva by marriage with Dora and comfort given to the blind old father. Picking up a paper dropped by Squire Harold, Dobson accuses him as the seducer of Eva, but Harold dodges the identification by displaying the Obituary Column of a newspaper announcing the decease of "Philip Edgar, of Toft Hall" (Harold's father). Dobson, in spite of the newspaper, resolves to keep an eye on Harold who "hasn't naw business 'ere wi' *my* Dora."

The third act supplies Climax but neither Dénouement nor Restoration of Order to the domestic tragedy. Dora, having set her house servant Milly to memorize a hymn about forgiveness—"forgive my mortal foe," turns to giving the farm hands their wages, involving a certain amount of rustic by-play. In the spirit of the hymn Dora forgives Dan Smith for theft of some coal, but admonishes him for spending all the previous week's wages at the ale-house. Sally Allen, who stopped working for Dobson because of his roughness, has lost her brother to what she calls the "Queen's Real Hard Tillery," but is planning on marriage to her sweetheart at Michaelmas. However she and two friends want to warn Dora that Philip Edgar has returned and that Sally could give positive identification because on his former visit "'A cotched ma about the waäist, Miss, when 'e wur 'ere afoor, an' axed ma to be 'is little sweet'art."

Dora soliloquizes that they are about at the end of their resources. The land will have to be sold and that would be the death of her father. Dobson, as husband, could save her but, like Sally, "I can't abide him;" compared to her Harold, he is "like a hedge thistle by a garden rose." She has evidently accepted his proposal of marriage but is troubled by his lack of Christian faith, and sings a song about happy larks and brooks compared with the Church tower and cemetery: "O Love and Life, how weary am I / And how I long for rest!" The woman bruised by Smith's cart is resting in the bedroom, identified by Dora, but not by her father or the farm hands. Dora even has dreams of her father and Eva living with them when she is Mrs. Harold! She vigorously defends her credentials for marriage to a gentleman: she reads, writes, talks French, plays the piano like a lady.

Dobson, with unusual finesse, sends blossoms from Miss Eva's garden to the bruised lady and asks to communicate something important to Dora, who claims she is too busy with her invalid guest to come. Eva is now well enough to tell about her rescue by a Sister of Mercy and her recommendation to seek forgiveness from her father before he dies. Dora thinks Eva's reappearance will give Farmer Steer "a new lease of life." But the blind father can think only of how hard he worked to rehabilitate the Steer family, and hearing Eva's voice, assumes he is distraught and shuffles out with Milly.

When Dora mentions *Pilgrim's Progress* to Harold, he asks, disdainfully, "That nursery-tale / Still read, then?" Religious cruelty has always been the enemy of the "common brotherhood of man." When she expresses doubt, for the first time, of being the fit wife of a gentleman, he replies that he had been called a socialist, Communist, Nihilist, but actually these false Utopias act only as the "soil / For Caesars, Cromwells, and Napoleons / To root their power in." Some observers gossip that he has abandoned such political theories because of inheritance from his uncle. Dora reminds Harold of the deep Saxon roots of both their families. He roughly rejects such pride, saying he inherited 3,000 acres, not a Saxon name (quite different from the importance of Saxon inheritance in Tennyson's drama, *Harold*). But he changes the subject when she asks what was his former name? We are all "poor earthworms" he naturalistically claims, "crawling in this boundless Nature." When he offers her marriage he says this is his first such offer, and that may indeed be true. But when he ardently insists that she is "the first / I ever have loved truly," Eva cries out from the next room where she has heard all: "Philip Edgar," and swaying in the doorway admonishes "Make her happy, then, and I forgive you," and promptly falls dead.

Harold's reaction is that all this was a charade worked out by the two sisters to make him confess his culpability. Quite unrepentant, Harold wonders "Were it best to steal away, to spare myself," and then, with crocodile tears adds belatedly:

> And her too, pain, pain, pain"
> My curse on all
> This world of mud, on all its idiot gleams
> Of Pleasure, all the foul fatalities
> That blast our natural passions into pains!

The audacity of Edgar cursing the world instead of himself is still sustained by his mechanistic philosophy—all he did was natural, to derive the Utilitarian sumum bonum of pleasure; how dare the world transform his pleasure into other's pains?

When Dobson appears to punish Edgar, the latter calls him "mere wild beast"—But Dora stands between and tells Dobson he is "tenfold more a gentleman, / A hundred times more worth a women's love." Then she summarizes Edgar's crimes: Eva was only fifteen "in the promise of her May," then five years of shame and suffering," and her father lost to health, eyesight, and mind. On top of that Edgar set out to seduce the second sister, but Edgar protests that indeed he does love her, even though his original intention of marrying Dora was to make amends to Eva and Farmer Steer. With the refrain "Nothing from you!" Dora claims homelessness and a pauper's death. In three succinct phrases she convicts the miscreant: she forgave you, I forgive you, but can you ever forgive yourself? If so, she pronounces, you are lower and baser "Than even I can well believe." He lies lowly at her feet and the curtain falls.

When *The Promise of May* began its five-week run November 1882 at the Globe Theatre of London, it may well have had a *succés de scandale*, because at an early presentation, the Marquis of Queensberry (famous for the Rules of Boxing and infamous for his attack on Oscar Wilde) arose, at the close of the play, to identify himself as a Freethinker and to denounce Tennyson's tragedy as a travesty on his intellectual liberalism. The next day he explained in a morning paper that he was particularly outraged by Philip Edgar's comments on marriage:

I am a secularist and a freethinker, and, though I repudiate it, a so-called atheist, and as President of the British Secular Union, I protest against Mr. Tennyson' abominable caricature of an individual whom, I presume he would have us believe represents some body of people which, thanks for the good of humanity, most certainly does not exist among freethinkers. (Rolfe pp. 731)

The stage manager must have calculated with delight the number of seats which would be filled by the fray, but the author was so much upset that his son Lionel attempted to set the record straight by publishing an analysis of the character of Edgar. The epigraph of the play itself had set the tone of Lionel's defense.—"A surface man of theories, true to none." Edgar is not,

as the critics will have it, a freethinker drawn into crime by his Communist theories; Edgar is not a protest against the atheism of the age; Edgar is not even an honest Radical nor a sincere follower of Schopenhauer; he is nothing thorough and nothing sincere; but he is a criminal, and at the same time a gentleman. These are the two sides of his character. He has no conscience until he is brought face to face with the consequences of his crime [and perhaps not even then!], and in the awakening of that conscience the poet has manifested his fullest and sublimest strength.

Yet a careful reading of the text does show Edgar as one of the intelligentsia, repeating passages from Locke, Godwin, Hume, and Mill in his conversations with his mistress Eva and in his rationalization of his own callous behavior. Darwin's references to man as animal nature and the survival of the fittest find place in his specious arguments. In Act III he even boasts that he has been "call'd a Socialist, / A Communist, a Nihilist" and so cannot be accused of supporting social conventions.

Tennyson's Protagonist in "Locksley Hall" 1842, like Edgar, speaks glowingly of "the vision of the world and all the wonder that would be." Like Edgar he rants against "the social wants that sin against the strength of youth;" "sickly forms that err from honest Nature's rule" sounds as if from Edgar's own lips. Like Edgar, he feels "wild pulsation" and longs for a humanistic "Parliament of man." Edgar would have cherished "what is that to him that reaps not harvest of his youthful joys?" He would certainly have agreed with "Locksley Hall's" classification of women:

women's pleasure, women's pain —
Nature made them blinder motions bounded in a shallower brain.
Woman is the lesser man and all thy passions, match'd with mine,
Are as moonlight unto sunlight, and as water unto wine —
[cf. "Locksley Hall Sixty Years After" and the
satyrs of *In Memoriam*]

Of course it is only fair to add that Tennyson had earlier in the XXXV Canto of *In Memoriam* 1850 written despairingly about mortal love unlinked with the hope of immortality:

Love had not been,
Or been in narrowest working shut
* * *
Mere fellowship of sluggish moods
Or in his coarsest Satyr-shape
Had bruised the herb and crush'd the grape,
And bask'd and batten'd in the woods.

Edgar was certainly outside the dimension of religious faith, but his womanizing seemed quite conventional and occasionally poetic compared with the wild, orgiastic world of satyrs. As the aged protagonist of "Locksley Hall Sixty Years After" 1886, the "modern amorist" (like Edgar) was of "easier, earthlier make." The world the young protagonist of "Locksley Hall" dreamed about, the "new age" Edgar already inhabited has come and left its inhabitants: "Gone the cry of 'Forward, Forward,' lost within a growing gloom:"

Half the marvels of my morning, triumphs over time and space,
Staled by frequence, shrunk by usage into commonest commonplace!

The protagonist of the second "Locksley Hall" would quite agree with Edgar's demeaning "Good day, then, Dobbins" to Farmer Dobson. Edgar is gentry, Farmers Steer and Dobson of lower mentality and emotion:

Envy wears the mask of Love, and, laughing sober fact to scorn,
Cries to weakest as to strongest; "Ye are equals, equal born."

Surely the rural setting of *The Promise of May* has taught its inhabitants, by the analogy of animal breeding, that quality animals require selective breeding. As Tennyson put it, are hill and plain equal, the lion no larger than a cat?

At the "importunate entreaty" of Sabine Greville (*Letters* III 233n) "*Do, Do* begin a Village Tragedy and leave that ungentlemanly old woman Queen Elizabeth alone," and recalling John Ruskin's eloquent plea to leave the Arthurian legend and describe the tragedies of contemporary life "with no one to write the tale," Tennyson, in the genre of *Enoch Arden* wrote *The Promise of May* 1882 as an experiment in dramatic prose. Henry Irving was not tempted; William Hunter and Madge Kendal, who had produced *The Falcon*, declined because the play was too brief! "It is full of dramatic incident and character, but. . . the dramatic incident and character are so *strong*, the whole requires to be much more fully developed!" (*Mem.* II 267)

But Mrs. Bernard Beere, having heard the Laureate read *The Promise of May* aloud, decided to produce and herself play the role of Dora: "The comedy touches alone, as you read them, ought to make a success of the piece. . . .I hope to be able to interpret it in a way that would please you" (October 7, *Mem.* II 266,7). Although the reasons for rejection were as specious as the reasons for acceptance, care and thought were lavishly bestowed on every detail of the production (Arthur Waugh, *Alfred Lord Tennyson*, 206).

When Mary Gladstone attended, November 11, 1882, "It was most painful there being a brutal Bradlaugh gallery and pit who jeered and hissed and greeted with peals of laughter the special points of pathos, morality or tragedy."

Even the choice of opening date was catastrophic. A columnist wrote about the problem of Saturday openings:

> . . . the most noisy, the most insolent, the most intolerant, the most cruel. People who came into the theatre for a spree are incapable of judging of a work of art. The Poet Laureate, poor innocent man! was led into a deep pitfall. The play that should have commenced at eight o'clock in order to please the people, was not started until a quarter past nine. The assembled audience had not. . .to do but kick their heels in the theatre, with nothing to amuse them but a comedietta played by two ladies, who did not rise above the level of amateurs. The patience of the audience was exhausted. . . .Overture after overture was played and hooted. When the overture proper began, it was not

listened to. . . . The theatre was overcrowded. People had forced their way into the pit and gallery, where they could not by any possibility see, and when the play was not found to be immediately satisfactory, the discontented, wearied, and overcrowded audience adopted ridicule as the easiest form of relief (*Theatre*, NS Nov. 1882, 366).

Alfred Tennyson's own reaction to all this chaos is contained in a letter to an unknown supporter, written in mid-November of 1882:

I am grateful for your letter. I have received others to the same purport. The English Drama is at its lowest ebb and the Dramatic Criticism (as far as I have seen it) follows the ebb instead of being that light which should lead it back to the flow.

I had a feeling that I would at least strive to bring the true Drama of character and life back again. I gave them one leaf out of the great book of truth and nature. In Germany it would have answered and perhaps it will here still. Who knows? That old sonnet of Milton came into my head when I heard of the ruffians in the gallery, who were, I dare say, set on by one who shall gain no credit from being named by me.

I did but prompt the age to quit their clogs (2nd Sonnet "On the Detraction which Followed upon My Writing Certain Treatises") their melodramas, their sensationalisms, their burlesque—burlesque, the true enemy of humour, the thin bastard sister of poetical caricature who I verily believe from her utter want of human feeling would in a revolution be the first to dabble her hands in blood.

When straight a barbarous noise environs me
Of owls and asses, cuckoos, apes and dogs —
But this is got by casting pearls to hogs.

On the whole, I think I am rather glad of the row for it shows that I have not drawn a bow at a venture.

Yours very truly
A. Tennyson

The person unnamed by the playwright was probably Queensberry, but obliquely Charles Bradlaugh, an advocate of free thought and the elected MP for Northampton (1880-91). When he attempted to take his seat in the House of Commons, he refused to swear an oath on the Bible, substituting a simple personal affirmation instead. An uproar ensued and in 1880 he was denied seating, in 1881 he was forcibly ejected from the House, controversy continued until finally the matter was resolved in his favor in 1886. It is worthy of note that Tennyson, so admired for his medieval and classical studies, here dared to throw himself actively into the contemporary drama of ideas. Edgar, before his inheritance, would surely have been sympathetic with the courageous stand of Bradlaugh, but Tennyson's portrayal suggests he would not dare to emulate his adamancy.

It is of double interest to hear Tennyson so roundly condemn the melodrama, sensationalisms, and burlesques that Charles Dickens loved, participated in, and transcribed in novelistic form. The other interest is to hear his claim to the diagnosis of character and the life-likeness of his own drama.

Despite Tennyson's high tone in regard to *The Promise of May*, the audience may well have been justified to see in Edgar a thinly-veiled attack upon Charles Bradlaugh and "horrible infidel writings? O yes, / For these are the new dark ages, you see, of the popular press" ("Despair," 1881, suggested to Tennyson by Mary Gladstone and parodied by Swinburne's "Disgust"). *The Promise of May* became part of Tennyson's oral repertoire and sometime, after one such private performance he snorted "And the papers called that a failure. . . .Why it's a perfect gem." Wickedly Mary diarized, "This he said, in the most naive way, and took our silence for consent."

When *Locksley Hall Sixty Years After Etc.* was published in December 1886, it included *The Promise of May*, which he had earlier asked Kegan Paul to withdraw from publication even though the proofs were ready to run. It can only have been because it matched the title poem in mood and subject and because they both bore a message he wanted the English people to hear (Thorn 498).

Chapter VIII

ℬ) Q

Two Short Plays:
The Falcon and *The Cup*

*T*he Falcon, produced by Mr. and Mrs. Henry Kendal at St. James'
Theatre in December of 1879, was so extremely short (592 lines,
only four characters) that it was usually presented in conjunction with
another play to provide a full Victorian evening of drama, and when
published in 1884 was combined with *The Cup*.

The source for Tennyson was undoubtedly the Ninth Tale, on the
Fifth Day of Giovanni Boccaccio's fourteenth century *Decameron*, itself
stemming from the Sanskrit Panchitranta. Its theme was well-known in
the West, providing the material for La Fontaine's "Le Faucon," *Contes
et Nouvelles*; Longfellow's "The Falcon of Ser Federigo," *Tales of the
Wayside Inn*; even dramatized as a three-act comedy by Delisle de la
Drévetière. With its dependence upon plot reversal and *la sommet fausse*,
Tennyson's 592 lines tend to be dominated by the Exposition of events in
the past, action only related and the dénouement unconvincing. R. Brimley
Johnson, in 1913, correctly describes the play as "an exquisite little
poem in action," putting his finger accurately upon its two poles of
dynamic, the plot that overwhelms characterization and the unusual

lushness of diction and omnipresence of symbolism. At the same time
the Laureate was writing this "bagatelle," he was also composing the
deep painfulness of "The Children's Hospital" and the heroic activism of
"The Voyage of Maeldune" and "Columbus." *Ca.* 1882 was a nightmare
period in which Tennyson's friends were passing away: his brother,
Spedding, Carlyle, Dean Stanley, Drummond Rawnsley, Longfellow,
and his neighbor in Freshwater, W.G. Ward, who frequently encouraged
and supported Tennyson in his doubtful musings about death and
immortality. Writing this Italian poem of love and sorrow thwarted by
cross purposes, he must often have identified with his own Columbus:

> you will tell the King, that I,
> Racked as I am with gout, and wrenched with pains
> Gained in the service of His Highness, yet
> Am ready to sail forth on one last voyage,
> And readier, if the King would hear, to lead
> One last crusade against the Saracen,
> And save the Holy Sepulchre from thrall.

Sailing an uncharted dramatic sea, he pressed on with valor and
determination. The year seemed appropriate in which to write a poem to
commemorate the nineteenth centenary of Virgil's death, including the
tell-tale lines: "Thou majestic in thy sadness / At the doubtful doom of
human mind."

The special lushness of diction is expressed immediately (line 4) in
the Count's rhapsody addressed to his falcon:

> My princess of the cloud, my plumed purveyor,
> My far-eyed queen of the winds — thou that canst soar
> Beyond the morning lark, and, howsoe'er
> The quarry wind and wheel, swoop down upon him
> Eagle-like, lightening-like — strike, make his feathers
> Glance in mid heaven.

Perhaps Tennyson wanted to mimic Italianate effusiveness rather than
British understatement, or, in a short poem dominated by plot activity,
he wished, like Keats, to "fill every rift with ore." But of the symbolic
underscoring of the falcon there can be no question. The bird is the one
thing of beauty left to the impoverished nobleman; it returns the affection
he bestows (unlike Lady Giovanna); as bird of prey it provides meat for

the frugal table; as companion it cheers his days like nothing else; like Christ, it will give its own life to assure the Count's happiness. But as entrée on the table, its lean, vulpine nature makes it an unappetizing or even comic feast.

The central plot reversal—the falcon killed to make lunch for the Lady when she has come to beg for the bird to heal her spoiled and ailing son—is the obvious parent of O'Henry's "Gift of the Magi," when wife has sacrificed her hair to buy a watch-chain for her husband, who has sold his watch to buy combs for her hair.

The wreath is the other central symbol. Given to fifteen-year-old Giovanna, lost by her in timorous flight, it becomes the representative of all precious gifts given in love, but not received. It is only in the middle of the play that Lady Giovanna suggests that it was not lost out of carelessness, but bashfulness to pick it up beneath the Count's eyes.

The cottage, of course, doubly symbolizes the poverty of the Count and the wealth, by contrast, of the Lady's Castle, as well as the Quixotic romantic gesture of selling off the Count's ancestral castle to make an anonymous gift of a diamond necklace to a lady who has jewels aplenty.

The central contrast of the little drama is the outrageous extravagant passion of the Lady's brother maintaining a family feud, the Lady unwilling to marry anyone because the Count she loves is a hereditary enemy, the spoiled boy pettishly demanding the last precious possession of the Count, and the Count, most of all, going to war because of a discarded wreath and exchanging his family patrimony for a bauble. By comparison there are two real human beings in the play, foster-brother Filippo and nurse Elisabetta. Amid the chaos of high-strung nerves and extravagant gestures, they wash the linen, prepare the food, and pawn the silver for daily bread. They are the Sancho Panza and Don Quixote's Aunt who make it possible for this Italian Quixote to joust with windmills. But Tennyson had his own characteristic earthiness, as when a lady dancing-partner told him that this was the greatest moment of her life and he replied that she must be out of her mind, or when invited to write a Christmas book he declined by likening it to milking he-goats providing neither honor nor profit. Surely he must have gasped in the high histrionic atmosphere of Count and Lady. Equally surely he must have relaxed with the service of Elisabetta and the funny but loyal antics of the Count's foster-brother.

Like many Tennyson poems, his lyric gift is exhibited by interspersed song. First Giovanna asks permission to read the scroll attached to the dried wreath, and then the Count, accompanying himself on the guitar, sings an unlikely lament entitled "Dead Mountain Flowers," continually interrupted by Elisabetta until the Count forgets his own song and must bring it to an awkward end. It is difficult to feel that Tennyson sets the good old dame on to break up the intolerable awkwardness of the situation. For once, the Laureate seems to prefer lunch to poetry—and such a lunch!

The Falcon played sixty-seven performances—a not inconsiderable run, but the audience often seemed more responsive to its companion piece, tending to use the former as a curtain-riser.

Contemporary critic J. Cuming Walters 1893, was contemptuous of the play: "its triviality of treatment and its staleness of subject would render it unmeet for serious criticism, even if it were redeemed by a single passage worthy of remembrance." However, he considered that the early plays (*Harold*, *Becket*, and *The Falcon*) "contained some of Tennyson's best thoughts and served as preparation for later dramas (*The Cup*, *The Promise of May*, and *The Foresters*)." The last he considered "the best of its class, the one of the least ambitious, it is almost a flawless piece of workmanship, in which he came near achieving absolute success" (Walters, 167ff).

The Cup

The Cup, begun November 1879, immediately after Tennyson's completion of *The Falcon*, was finished by 1880. Produced by an enthusiastic Irving (who played Synorix to Ellen Terry's Camma), it began its run at the Lyceum Theatre January 3, 1881 and played for approximately 130 nights (*Memoir* 130, Viscount Charles Eversley notes 128, Austin Brereton 127, Ellen Terry 125), thus becoming Tennyson's longest running play in England (longer runs in America) and perhaps his greatest stage success. Both *The Falcon* and *The Cup* were published by Macmillan in 1884.

Tennyson was not particularly pleased by Irving's playing of Synorix. "Irving has not hit off my Synorix, who is a subtle blend of Roman refinement and intellectuality, and barbarian, self-satisfied sensuality" (*Memoir* II 258 n.2).

4 Upper Belgrave Street
February 26, 1881

My dear Camma

You did it beautifully — not only the wifely and tender part of the character, but the talk about the patriots and the cry to the Goddess, which, if I recollect rightly, you had some fear of falling short in. As for the two or three passages which I thought might be more emphasized [I ii 214-30; II 70-74, 160-182], don't think of altering them in the acting — it would only confuse you — not at least till I see you again. . . . I was so entranced that I lost my spectacles — my reading ones — I heard them fall and forgot to pick them up. I trust the boxkeeper will find them.

Yours joyfully
A. Tennyson

I must add one line to say that my father told me that he was "very much impressed by your inspired earnestness." (H.T.)

Mary Gladstone found the January 11 performance "very short, very exciting and horrible, very exciting in stage effects and here and there fine in writing"—thus matching on the stage the Victorian appetite for such "sensation" novelists as Wilkie Collins and Charles Reade. But her estimate of Terry's acting was somewhat divided: "it is beautiful, though scarcely powerful enough. It is more perfection of grace than tragic power" (*Letters* III 206 n.).

She was sufficiently fascinated by the play that she attended another performance on February 26: "Went again to *The Cup* and *The Corsican Brothers*. Thought the former boundlessly beautiful. It grows wonderfully" (*M.G. Diaries* 215-6). Because of *The Cup's* brevity it was generally double-billed, on this first occasion with Dion Boucicault's adaptation of the Dumas novel.

Tennyson's little tragedy was itself adapted from Plutarch's *De Mulier, Virt.* via W.E.H. Lecky's *A History of European Morals* (342, 1894 ed.).

Few alterations were found necessary for the acting version, although the Laureate was unusually lamb-like about offering to do so: "My father will alter anything — or pray omit any of the lines which you think superfluous" (*Letters* III 202), acting not only as amanuensis but also as intermediary. In point of fact, the emendations generally took the form of expansions rather than contractions of the already miniature jewel.

A signal success at the Lyceum, playing always to crowded houses, Irving had arranged for James Thomas Knowles to design the second act Temple Scene upon archeological floor plans for the Great Temple of Diana; Alex Murray of the British Museum advised on Early Etruscan motifs, and three acclaimed dramatic painters of the period prepared the scenery which the Prime Minister's daughter found so splendid.

The sensational structure of the plot is based upon the reversals dear to the French theatre: Synorix begins as Tetrarch of Galilee expelled by his own people, becomes Tetrarch by courtesy of Rome, marries the widowed Camma and dies of poison on his wedding day; Sinnatus, happily married to Camma, welcomes Synorix (under a pseudonym) to a stag hunt, dabbles in conspiracy to throw off the Roman yoke, follows Camma to assignation with Antonius for forgiveness of her husband, is set upon by Publius and ten soldiers, slain by Synorix with the very knife Camma brought for self-protection. Camma will do anything for her beloved husband, including begging forgiveness for her husband's simplistic conspiracy, consenting to marry her husband's killer, poisoning the wedding cup to assure both his and her deaths. Antonius who hates dealing with the bestial Synorix but finds him useful to Rome, first assists then agrees to the rightfulness of his death. Even the knife and cup undergo reversals: the knife to protect Camma's honor becomes the weapon with which her husband's throat is slit; the cup from Artemis' Temple, given by Synorix as a pre-nuptial gift to Camma, becomes the poisoned vessel by which Synorix dies. The cup itself is part of a double reversal. Rescued originally by Synorix from a shrine of Artemis burned by the Roman army, and presented to Camma, "it is the cup we use in our marriages" (I i 25). But in Act II Camma shows Synorix a more authentic cup; many hundreds of years old with "The many-breasted mother Artemis / Emboss'd upon it" (II, 196). It is worthy of note that Artemis of the great temple at Ephesus was an Asiatic fertility goddess, not the sister of Apollo and the patroness of chastity. So the authentic cup would have a figure like a pineapple covered with sixty-some breasts, tapering down to an engraved pedestal. The cup given by Synorix to Camma would have been a more decorous representation of the goddess.

It is interesting that ten years later the Rev. E.H. Perowne, master of Corpus Christi College, Cambridge was writing about the Galatians as background for Paul's epistle. He reminds readers that the Galatians were Phrygian invaders from the highland of Armenia, given to worship of Cybele with orgiastic music and wild dancing, Celts connected racially to the Gaul who sacked Rome in the 4th century B.C. Both Julius Caesar and Tacitus described Galatians as restless, impulsive and fickle, so fierce that whole tribes hired out as mercenaries. It was the outcry of the silversmiths, marshaled by Demetrius in the city stadium, "Great is Diana of the Ephesians" (Acts 19), for more than two hours, that made it impossible for Paul either to placate the mob or preach the Gospel.

It is not difficult to understand the enormous popularity of the character Camma for the Victorian theater-goer. Her husband Sinnatus is described as "a rough, bluff, simple-looking fellow," but Camma loves him with extraordinary devotion. She will venture, with only a woman's dagger, into an encampment of Romans to save his life. As widow, she seeks refuge with priestesses of Artemis and will not re-marry even to become Queen. She is capable of devising a self-immolative scheme which will result in her own death in order to poison her husband's assassin exactly at the apogée of his accession to the throne and wedding to the former Queen.

This is a play with a heroine and without a hero—splendid, daring, and utterly loyal like the sensation novelist Charles Reade's contrast between splendid Juno figures and clinging-vine Phoebes. The villain, Synorix is accused by his Roman ally Antonius as "Hot-blooded! I have heard them say in Rome / That your own people cast you from their bounds / for some unprincely violence to a woman." But Synorix boasts "I ever had my victories among women," and in a Victorian melodramatic aside Antonius spits out his disgust: "I hate the man! / What filthy tools our Senate works with! Still / I must obey them [*aloud.*] Fare you well."

When one consults the subject-index of my book on Charles Reade (Simon and Schuster, 1976) I find references to the Juno-Phoebe contrast in heroines in not less than six of his novels. In *Christie Johnstone*, the heroine is described as one of those women who "had a grand corporeal tract; they had never known a corset, so they were straight as javelins; they could lift their hands above their heads! — actually" (Chapter II). And in *A Terrible Temptation* the dove (Phoebe) becomes the falcon (Juno) when her mother is affronted by a male attorney: "The towering threat and the flaming eye and the swift rush buffeted the caitiff away: he recoiled, she followed him as he went, strong, for a moment or two, as Hercules, beautiful and terrible as Michael driving Satan" (Chapter IV).

Thus, when Camma has poisoned her husband's slayer and herself, she watches his last struggles unperturbed: "So falls the throne of an hour," and when he reminds her that she too is coming his way of poisoned death, she exults: "Thy way? poor worm, crawl down thine own black hole / To the lowest hell" (II 276). So Camma joins the host of strong Victorian heroines victorious over vicious and weak males, including such disparate figures as Wilde's Lady Bracknell, and Shaw's St. Joan.

Chapter IX

ဆၣလ

Two Outdoor Plays:
Tennyson, *The Foresters*;
Wordsworth, *The Borderers*

"At liberty to act on their own impulses" Wordsworth

When Tennyson was deep in the composition of *Becket*, he wrote a sonnet as a Preface:

> Old ghost whose day was done ere mine began,
> If earth be seen from your conjectured heaven,
> Ye know that History is half-dream—ay even
> The man's life in the letters of the man.
> There lies the letter, but it is not he
> As he retires into himself and is:
> Sender and sent-to go to make up this,
> Their offspring of this union. And on me
> Frown not, old ghosts, if I be one of those
> Who make you utter things you did not say,
> And mould you all awry and mar your worth;
> For whatsoever knows us truly, knows

That none can truly write his single day,
And none can write it for him upon earth.
                              (*Works*, vol. 9, p. 415)

The "old ghosts" of Robin Hood and his merry men were to be dramatized on the stage for a historical purpose in Tennyson's epic studies of the Making of England. "In 'The foresters,' I have sketched the state of the people in another great transition period of the making of England, when the barons sided with the people and eventually won for them the Magna Carta" (*Memoir* II Chapter VIII p. 173). In a way, this is his "sartor resartus" whereby he starts with a legendary twelfth century aristocrat-outlaw figure famous for robbing the rich to help the poor. The Earl of Huntingdon had already been transformed into the forest outlaw folk-hero who lived in Sherwood Forest with his chief archer Little John, his chaplain Friar Tuck, his mistress Maid Marian and an assorted band. As such, he became the hero of at least thirty Middle English ballads, *Piers Plowman*, the Victorian *Ivanhoe*, and the late twentieth century *The Once and Future King*.

Instead of the mere entertainment of a merry tale for boys of all ages, Tennyson will transform, according to his own stated intention, the Earl of Huntingdon from a Robin Hood robbing the rich to aid the poor to a baronial leader who sides with the poor peasants and yeomen to eventually win for them the Magna Carta limiting the powers of both tyrannical king and oppressive barons.

Written in 1870 and published in 1881, Tennyson's *The Foresters* was not performed until March 17, 1892 at Daly's Theatre in New York City. The playwright died on October 6 that same year. Although the performance was in America, Sir Arthur Sullivan composed the incidental music for this play so full of interspersed songs that it might almost be considered a musical comedy. The American reception was enthusiastic, the house was always packed and the run was long and successful. Indeed it moved on to Washington, Baltimore, Philadelphia, Chicago, and Boston, "everywhere received with great enthusiasm" (W.J. Rolfe).

At Baltimore Professor Richard Claverhouse Jebb on his way to lecture at Johns Hopkins, saw the presentation.

The Theatre, which is of moderate size, was densely packed, and as I had not engaged my seat by cablegram from Liverpool, I bore no resemblance, in respect of spacious comfort, to the ideal spectator, the masher or "dude," depicted on the play-bill which I send you by this post. I was a highly compressed and squalid object in a back seat, amid a seething mass of humanity, but I saw the play very well. It was very cordially received and was well acted, I thought, especially by Ada Rehan and Drew. The fairy scene in the third Act was perfectly lovely, and the lyrics were everywhere beautifully given. The mounting of the play was excellent throughout.

(Memoir II, 397)

In regard to the "fairy scene," Tennyson was not particularly confident.

I don't care for *The Foresters* as I do for *Becket* and *Harold.* Irving suggested the fairies in my Robin Hood, else I should not have dreamed of trenching on Shakespeare's ground in that way. Then Irving wrote to me that the play was not "sensational" enough for an English public. It is a woodland play—a pastoral without shepherds. The great stage-drama is wholly unlike most of the drama of modern times. I do not like the idea of every scene being obliged to end with a *bang. (Works* 532)

In regard to the chorus "There is no land like England," Hallam said his father was particularly pleased by the comment of Horace Furness of Philadelphia (eminent Shakespeare scholar) in a letter to Lady Martin (Helen Faucit) written during the play's New York run.

After dinner we went to see "The Foresters." Men and women of a different time, to be sure, but none too good "for human nature's daily food"—live their idyllic lives before you, and you feel that all is good, very good. The atmosphere is so real, and we fall into it so completely, that, Americans though we be through and through, we can listen with hearty assent to the chorus that "There is no land like England," and that "There are no wives like English wives." Nay, come to think of it, that song was encored. It was charming, charming from beginning to end. And Miss Rehan acted to perfection. I had to leave in the midnight train for home, and during two hours' driving through the black night, I smoked and reflected on the unalloyed charm of such a drama. And to see the popularity, too! It had been running many weeks—six, I think—and the theatre was full, not a seat unoccupied. I do revel, I confess, in such a proof as this that there will always be a full response to what is fine and good, and that the modern sensational French drama is not our true exponent. *(Memoir* II, 397)

Much of the acclaim accorded the pastoral in America was in the form of admiration for the leading lady, Ada Rehan. She, in turn, graciously returned the compliments to the playwright.

> Let me add my congratulations to the many on the success of *The Foresters*. I cannot tell you how delighted I was when I felt and saw, from the first, the joy it was giving to our large audience. Its charm is felt by all. Let me thank you for myself for the honour of playing your *Maid Marian*, which I have learned to love, for while I am playing the part I feel all its beauty and simplicity and sweetness, which make me feel for the time a happier and a better woman. I am indeed proud of its great success for your sake as well as my own.
>
> P.S.—The play is now one week old, and each audience has been larger than the last and all as sympathetic as the first. (*Works*, vol. 9, 530)

Somehow the interspersed songs seem less jarring and out of place in the garden setting of Sir Richard Lea's castle (Act I, scene i) and Sherwood Forest than in the stately historical dramas set in the courts of kings. For example, the most successful songs of *Becket* are sung in Rosalind's woodland Bower with a little lad playing nearby.

"The Warrior Earl of Allendale" moves with the pace of medieval folk ballads in four/three time. Fighting and loving serve as analogues to each other. "Love Flew in at the Window" plays a moralistic little game in which inconstant Wealth, or its absence, is overcome by the faithfulness of love, in high Victorian two-stanza lyrics rhyming abccb in both stanzas of three-foot anapaestic lines broken by the cc couplet of four feet. The drinking song "Long Live Richard, Down with John" successfully handles rhymed two-foot lines that sound exactly like toasts at a banquet. "To Sleep!" (I, iii) was first published in *New Review* 1891 and set to music by Lady Tennyson (*Works*, vol. 9, p. 532). The mood is curiously broken between the longer cadences of

> Whate'er thy joys, they vanish with the day.
> Whate'er thy griefs, in sleep they fade away

five times broken by the brief, harsh exordium "To Sleep! To Sleep!" Like nineteenth century hymns the end of the poem deals with death and eternity: "Sleep, happy soul! all life will sleep at last."

Act II appropriately begins with a patriotic "Working Song," "There is no land like England," which celebrates English hearts, men, maids, and wives," joining in the Full Chorus:

> And these will fight for England
> And man and maid be free
> To foil and spoil the tyrant
> Beneath the green wood tree.

It is of interest that Hallam and Lord Tennyson lodged in Sherwood Forest during the composition of the play and thus some of the happy enthusiasm of the actual setting flows over into the mood on the stage as the "mourning muse" of England reverts to cheerful and brisk celebration of a history in which freedom is won. To be sure of the contagion, Tennyson "recommended [Augustin] Daly to look at Whymper's pictures of Sherwood Forest, which he straightway bought in order that they might be copied for the scenes" (*Works*, vol. 9, p. 532).

The Fairy Scene, written by Tennyson for the end of Act II, but moved to the end of Act III for greater effectiveness on the stage, was suggested by Irving somewhat against the author's plan. These fairies complain to Queen Titania that humans have made their refuge in the Forest impossible:

> We be scared with song and shout.
> Arrows whistle all about.
> All our games be put to rout.
> All our rings be trampled out.
> Lead us thou to some deep glen.
> Far from solid foot of men,
> Never to return again

Titania accedes to their plea: "adieu for ever and for evermore—adieu." Oberon had already departed; Titania will now lead away her fairy nation and a frolicsome harmlessness will depart from a disenchanted England.

Little John and Will Scarlet have composed a song in honor of Robin and Marian in which the first stanza ends roguishly, "We care so much for a King;/ We care not much for a Queen." When Marian protests, the whole group amend the second stanza to end "We care so much for a King / That we would die for a Queen!"

Marian's "The Bee buzz'd up in the Heat" (Act IV, sc. i) is an example of Tennyson's rather awkward peasant humor, suggesting that the bee loses interest in the blossom once it is faded and honeyless— "And that the bee buzz'd off in the cold."

The dance of the Abbot and Justiciary follows their extortion of Sir Richard's bond: 1,000 marks to release his land, an interest ("for use") charge which immediately rises from 400 to 500 marks once the Justiciary realized Robin will pay whatever is asked, with the final (they think) indignity of forfeiture of the land for lateness: "these monies should be paid in to the Abbot at York, at the end of the month at noon, and they are delivered here in the wild wood an hour after noon" (Act IV, sc. i). When Marian plaintively queries: "Have you no pity?" the Justiciary appositively replies "What pity have you for your game?" Then he sets up his own final insult by impatiently asking "What? must we dance attendance all the day?" The verb suggested must become the verb acted and Abbot (with gout) and Justiciary (with varicose veins in his right leg) must dance or have calves pricked by arrow-points held by Robin's Band in a special form of merriment. Music strikes up and dance they must!

With the return of King Richard (in disguise) and Walter Lea (Sir Richard's son who escapes from prison), the gold for his ransom returned by an honest sailor who thinks he has failed in his quest, Maid Marian, soon to wed the restored Earl of Huntingdon, announces gala celebration, drinking, dining and the comedy closes with Song and Country Dance:

> Now the King is home again, and nevermore to roam again.
> Now the King is home again, the King will have his own again,
> Home again, home again, and each will have his own again,
> All the birds in merry Sherwood sing and sing him home again.

a marvelous example to remind us that Tennyson's much vaunted lyric impulse is firmly based on implacable repetition!

Maid Marian comes across as the unquestioned heroine of the pastoral drama, when, Boadicea-like, she defends her father and her honor—with Robin standing out of the footlights as a mere back-up!

> MARIAN (*drawing the bow*).
>
> No nearer to me! back! My hand is firm,
> Mine eyes most true to one hair's breadth of aim.
> You, Prince, our king to come—you that dishonour

The daughters and wives of your own faction—
Who hunger for the body, not the soul—
This gallant Prince would have me of his—what?
Household? or shall I call it by that new term
Brought from the sacred East, his harem? Never,
Tho' you should queen me over all the realms
Held by King Richard, could I stoop so low
As mate with one that holds no love is pure,
No friendship sacred, values neither man
Nor woman save as tools—God help the mark—
To his own unprincely ends. And you, you, Sheriff,
Who thought to buy your marrying me with gold,
Marriage is of the soul, not of the body.
Win me you cannot, murder me you may,
And all I love, Robin, and all his men,
For I am one with him and his; but while
I breathe Heaven's air, and Heaven looks down on me,
And smiles at my best meanings, I remain
Mistress of mine own self and mine own soul,
                    [Retreating, with bow drawn, to the bush.]
Robin!
                    ROBIN
          I am here, my arrow on the cord.
He dies who dares to touch thee. (Act IV, sc. i)

The pastoral theme runs consistently throughout—the Forest represents rude Saxon virtue against the sophisticated Norman knavery of castle and town. The handsome climax in the woods would certainly have been whittled away by petty complaints and obstruction in the town courts. No wonder Marian, in exasperation, cries "O God, I would the letter of the law / Were some strong fellow here in the wild wood. / That thou mightest beat him down at quarterstaff!" (*Works*, IX, 387).

Robin clearly takes second place to his doughty beloved, being cast as a melancholy, love-sick youth. Once again Marian makes the rhetorical comparison:

The Sheriff dare to love me? me who worship Robin the great Earl of Huntingdon? I love him as a damsel of his day might have loved Harold the Saxon, or Hereward the Wake. They both fought against the tyranny of the kings, the Normans. But then your Sheriff, your little man, if he dare to fight at all, would fight for his rents, his leases, his houses, his monies, his oxen, his dinners, himself. Now your great man, your Robin, all England's Robin, fights not for himself but for the People of England. This John—this Norman tyranny—the stream is bearing us all down and our little Sheriff will ever swim with the stream! but our great man, our Robin, against it. And how often in old histories have the great men striven against the stream and how often in the long sweep of years to come must the great man strive against it again to save his country, and the liberties of his people! God bless our well-beloved Robin, Earl of Huntingdon. (*Works*, 9, p. 267)

Robin himself, more thoughtful and less declamatory than Marian, makes a measured assessment of Prince John and recognizes the barons' threat of unbridled feudalism, perhaps even hinting at Tennyson's monarchist reservations concerning Magna Carta itself!

> But if it be so we must bear with John.
> The man is able enough—no lack of wit,
> And apt at arms and shrewd in policy.
> Courteous enough too when he wills; and yet
> I hate him for his want of chivalry.
> He that can pluck the flower of maidenhood
> From off the stalk and trample it in the mire,
> And boast that he hath trampled it. I hate him,
> I hate the man. I may not hate the King
> For aught I know,
> So that our Barons bring his baseness under.
> I think they will be mightier than the king.

The Sheriff of Nottingham occupies a somewhat central position between the philandering with women and the political corruption of John as over against a rather professional attitude toward his own job. Unlike the Prince who wants a wedding night with Marian (*droit de seigneur*) before he passes her over to the Sheriff, the Sheriff loves Marian and would like to marry her. He warns her against the entrapment by Prince John and offers to pay off Sir Richard's debt if she will "cast / An eye of favour on me." When Prince John commands his men to seize the girl and carry her off to *his*—castle, the Sheriff is outraged: "She is mine. I have thy promise." The Prince replies "O ay, she shall be thine—first mine, then thine, / For she shall spend her honeymoon with me." To which the chagrinned sheriff can only mutter: "Woe to the land shall own thee for her king!"

Tennyson's portrait of Richard the Lionhearted seems tinged with his "Ulysses" evasion of civil duty:

> It little profits that an idle king,
> By this still hearth, among these barren crags,
> Match'd with an aged wife, I mete and dole
> Unequal laws unto a savage race,
> That hoard, and sleep, and feed, and know not me.
>
> ("Ulysses" 1842)

Just as the Greek hero was willing to cede the conduct of his Kingdom, Ithaca, to his son Telemachus, in order that the father may be free for "roaming with a hungry heart," so Richard, for the sake of the Crusades, turned his kingdom, England, over to Prince John. In *The Foresters*, the indictment is made by Friar Tuck:

> Geese, man! for how canst thou be thus allied
> With John, and serve King Richard save thou be
> A traitor or a goose? but stay with Robin;
> For Robin is no scatterbrain like Richard,
> Robin's an outlaw, but he helps the poor.
> While Richard hath outlaw'd himself, and helps
> Nor rich, nor poor.
>   * * *
>   this Richard sacks and wastes a town
> With random pillage, but our Robin takes
> From whom he knows are hypocrites and liars.
> Again this Richard risks his life for a straw,
> So lies in prison—while our Robin's life
> Hangs by a thread, but he is a free man.
> Richard, again, is king over a realm
> He hardly knows, and Robin king of Sherwood,
> And loves and doats on every dingle of it.
> Again this Richard is the lion of Cyprus,
> Robin, the lion of Sherwood—may this mouth
> Never suck grape again, if our true Robin
> Be not the nobler lion of the twain.

However, King Richard, returning to England in disguise, becomes *deus ex machina* punishing villains and releasing honest men. It is his return that changes a civil tragedy into utopian comedy, but the two romantic plots (Little John/Kate; Robin/Maid Marian) have already achieved a loving tone and the pastoral setting of Sherwood Forest an atmosphere of light-hearted innocence. This must be what a late contemporary, J. Cuming Walters had in mind when he described *The Foresters* as "the last and best of its class, the one of the least ambitious, it is almost a flawless piece of workmanship—an idyll glowing with colour, a poem sparkling and spontaneous, a drama skillful and impressive."

In point of construction, the romantic comedy is a series of confrontations: Sir Richard Lea versus the Sheriff, the Abbot and the Justiciary; Little John versus Kate; Robin Hood versus Maid Marian; Saxon versus Norman; the town versus the forest; aristocracy versus monarchy; true religion versus false; the government of England versus the Holy land Crusades. The last confrontation is most reminiscent of King Arthur's reaction when he is told his Round Table has vowed to go on quest of the Holy Grail:

> his face
> Darken'd as I have seen it more than once. . .
>
> "Woe is me, my knights," he cried,
> "Had I been here, ye had not sworn the vow.
> Was I too dark a prophet when I said
> To those who went upon the Holy Quest
> That most of them would follow wandering fires,
> Lost in a quagmire? —lost to me and gone,
> And left me gazing at a barren board
> And a lean order . . ."

In the *Idylls of the King*, the twin malefactors are excessive sensual attraction and excessive religious zeal. And Friar Tuck claims that "this Richard risks his life for a straw, / So lies in prison" (IV, I). Richard replies (in behalf of himself):

> he flung
> His life, heart, soul into those holy wars
> That sought to free the tomb-place of the King
> Of all the world. (*Works* IX 382)

But the voice of Arthur from the ghostly past rejects his high claim:

> the King must guard
> That which he rules, and is but as the hind

To whom a space of land is given to plow,
Who may not wander from the allotted field
Before his work is done. (901-903)

So the medieval voice diagnoses the trouble with twelfth century England
as primarily that its true king would not stay home, but "wander from
the allotted field / Before his work is done"!

The Borderers, William Wordsworth

Like *The Foresters* by Tennyson, William Wordsworth's *The
Borderers* is set almost entirely out of doors. Composed at Racedown in
1795, about the time Wordsworth was recovering from his emotional
infatuation with the French Revolution and his intellectual thralldom to
Godwinism (Smith, *William Godwin*), it was not published until 1842,
eight years before Tennyson succeeded him as Poet Laureate.

William Godwin, in *An Enquiry Concerning the Principles of Political
Justice*, 1793, had argued that the chief obstacle to universal benevolence
was the particular affection for a single individual—My Wife, My Son,
My Life, etc. In a limited sense, Edgar, in *The Promise of May*, was a
Godwinite who cared much for the future of the human race, but nothing
for the individuals he manipulated and discarded. On the other hand,
Oswald, in *The Borderers*, has so great an affinity for evil that he becomes
an Iago figure spewing out his self-hatred on every life he touches. Set
in the reign of Henry III, 1216-72, a time of border disputes between
England and Scotland, "little more was required for my purpose," wrote
Wordsworth, "than the absence of established law and government, so
that the agents might be at liberty to act on their own impulses" (I, p.
108). Wordsworth was both personally and as playwright interested in
what can make the "apparently *motiveless* actions of bad men intelligible
to careful observers" (I, 109). He had just composed his long poetical
treatment of the subject—"Guilt and Sorrow, or Incidents upon Salisbury
Plain" (74 nine-line stanzas) and his fellow-poet Samuel Taylor Coleridge
had likewise been engaged in writing his tragedy, *Remorse*, on the similar
topic of the social consequences of evil actions by men usually considered
to be superior. Wordsworth was dismayed that his own poetic exploration
of human nature "suggests that awful truth . . . sin and crime are apt to
start from their very opposite qualities, so there are no limits to the

hardening of the heart, and the perversion of the understanding to which they may carry their slaves."

Both dramas were rejected for performance by Mr. Harris, the manager of Covent Garden, although Coleridge's *Remorse* was performed several years later through the kind intermediacy of Mr. Sheridan. Wordsworth never expected the acceptance of his tragedy for public performance, although he wryly confessed: "a successful play would in the then state of my finances have been a most welcome piece of good fortune" (I, 109).

Having been a witness to the beginning of the French Revolution and having been forced by his guardians' adamant command to return to England at once, the idealistic poet had to leave behind a pregnant French mistress. Thus in the drama he is engrossed by psychological-societal examination:

> My care was almost exclusively given to the passions and the characters, and the position in which the persons in the drama stood relatively to each other that the reader (for I thought of the stage at the time it was written) might be moved, and to a degree instructed, by lights penetrating somewhat into the depths of our nature. (I, 108)

In writing his historical comedy, Tennyson had turned to the rather cheerful, pastoral subject of Robin Hood and Maid Marian, but always with his chief focus on history rather than personality. "In 'The Foresters,' I have sketched the state of the people in another great transition period of the making of England, when the barons sided with the people and eventually won for them the Magna Charta'" (*Memoir* II, 173). Wordsworth, on the other hand, tells us almost nothing about the Border skirmishes between Scotland and England, but focuses his searchlight brilliantly on the pattern of how and why an Iago dupes a military leader with the resulting deaths of Desdomona, Iago, and Othello. Actually uncertain of his general knowledge of the Border Wars, Wordsworth boned up on Redpath's *History of the Borders*, but found it very tepid stuff: "I once made an observation to Sir W. Scott, in which he concurred, that it was difficult to conceive how so dull a book could be written on such a subject" (I, 109).

Marmaduke, ill-fated hero of *The Borderers*, despite the adulation of his courageous Band, is an early hero of the twentieth century type, to whom everything happens and by whom very little is done (Campbell, *Hero with a Thousand Faces*). His fatal flaw that inevitably draws him down from high place is his extraordinary vulnerability to the subtle suggestions of the tempter-villain Oswald. Deeply in love with Idonea, he supinely accepts the idea that his betrothed is heading for a ruined castle on the moor to give herself to the voluptuary, Sir Clifford, at her father's bidding, just as Sir Richard Lea wanted to barter Maid Marian to the Sheriff of Nottingham in return for the land he had put up as bond for ransom of his son. Deeply annoyed by Herbert's disapproval of his suit for his daughter, he swallows the testimony of a female vagabond (bribed by Oswald) that Idonea is not truly Herbert's child, and her supposed father is simply her pander, ready to repair his damaged fortune by sale of the adopted waif to the highest bidder. All observation should have proved Herbert to be a devoted father and Idonea the purest of maidens. But the serpent-whisper in his ear expunges all the clear testimony of his eyes. Herbert is physically blind, but like Tiresias, a model of clear-sightedness compared to the psychologically-blind hero. Maid Marian had found herself in the same bind in *The Foresters*: "My father's land can be saved only by my marriage to a man I despise."

Marmaduke's Border Band has figured out Oswald to be "the proud soul" to whom "gratitude [is] a heavy burden" because Marmaduke had once saved Oswald's life. A specious explanation compared with the twin observations of Marmaduke's true friends; first, Oswald is the kind of man to whom "strong feelings are natural" (Act I), and second that Oswald can only be fulfilled by complete and venomous control over his savior's life (Act III). "Power is life to him / And breath and being; where he cannot govern, / He will destroy" (Act III, scene 4). Thus Oswald is an effective but less puissant Prince John from *The Foresters*. And Marmaduke is correct in sensing Herbert's disapproval. Like many a solicitous parent, Herbert calls the Band "outlaws," and regrets that "My child . . . had given her love to a wild Freebooter / Who here upon the borders of the Tweed, / Doth prey alike on two distracted countries, / Traitor to both" (Act I, scene i).

In actual practice even Oswald notices the even-handed benevolence of Captain Marmaduke: and in an extraordinary moment of confession exclaims: "Your single virtue has transformed a Band / Of fierce barbarians into Ministers / Of peace and order" (II, i). This immediately reminds us of Robin Hood transforming the predatory lives of forest men into acts of ruthlessness for the rich, and charity for the poor (*The Foresters*).

But as Oswald infects Marmaduke with his lies and twists his deeds by careful manipulation, we see the candid good nature eroded by suspicions and doubts. The sneers of the tempter attack even his benevolence:

> Benevolence, that has not the heart to use
> The wholesome ministry of pain and evil
> Becomes at last weak and contemptible. (I, I)

Frankly confessing his growing dubiety, Marmaduke pleads with Oswald to note his slippery condition:

> Oswald, the firm foundation of my life
> Is going from under me; these strange discoveries
> Looked at from every point of fear or hope,
> Duty, or love—involve, I feel, my ruin (I, I).

Oswald's only response is to celebrate a fierce antinomianism: "Happy are we, / Who live in these disputed tracts, that own / No law but what each man makes for himself," echoing the anarchic epitaph of the Book of Judges: "every man did that which was right in his own eyes" (21:25).

Indeed Marmaduke's growing dubiety is robbing him of the capacity to act decisively. Lacy warns him that King Henry's reinstatement of ousted barons will require the Band's increased vigilance to "Defend the innocent." But the Band's captain now questions even their own patriotism. Are they not simply activists on the "surfaces of things," who, when they hear about human atrocities, "grasp our swords and rush upon a cure / That flatters us, because it asks not thought." Oswald's counsel has led him to think that the "deeper malady is better hid; / The world is poisoned at the heart" (I, iii). He even drags in Platonism to justify the murder of a blind old man; "I did believe all things were shadows—yea, / Living or dead all things were bodiless." This combination of dubieties leads Marmaduke to what he calls the cornerstone of his philosophy:

> I would not give a denier for the man
> Who, on such provocation as this earth
> Yields, could not chuck his babe beneath the chin
> And send it with a fillip to its grave. (III, i)

And Oswald congratulates him as an "independent intellect" (like Edgar in *The Promise of May*).

If Marmaduke is the manipulated victim, Idonea is the innocent victim. She loves Marmaduke; her father needs the support of Sir Clifford; the King's reinstatement of Herbert to his barony will make possible her union with Marmaduke. Little does she realize that her beloved, seduced by Oswald's lies, but unable to deliver the stroke of death to Baron Herbert, has more characteristically abandoned him to death on the moor by starvation and exposure.

The consequences of Oswald's poison are the death by stabbing at the hands of the Band, Idonea's adoption for their caretaking, and Marmaduke a wanderer appeasing the anger of heaven and waiting until "Mercy give me leave to die!" *The Foresters* ended with all human options open; *The Borderers* with all human options closed.

Conclusion

ဆာဂ

I t is perfectly clear that Alfred, Lord Tennyson would not agree to an easy dismissal of his drama.

When he set up the magnificent proposal of examining in drama the "making of England" by focusing on four critical historic junctures, he must, self-consciously have been adding his chronicle-dramas to the historical dramas of Shakespeare. William Shakespeare's historical drama, which he also might well have called an epic history of England, included: *King John, Richard II, Richard III, Henry IV* (1 and 2), *Henry V, Henry VI*.

Tennyson certainly agreed with Shakespeare on the significance of King John and *Magna Carta*, 1215 and used him as villain of *The Foresters*. Although Shakespeare's list included Henry VI and the beginning of the War of the Roses, and Richard III and the end of that feudal struggle, as well as Henry V and Agincourt, it seems more oriented toward the family dynasties of the Richards and the Henrys than a systematic examination of the pivotal points from which the English nation emerged.

Far more systematically, Tennyson chose *Harold* (1022-1066) the last Saxon king, to delineate that eventual amalgamation of Danish, Norman, Saxon and Angle which produced the British character. *Becket* (1133-1189) describes that struggle between crozier and crown which, in the drama, seems to award the prize to the Church, but in the long historical perspective to the Crown. *Mary* (1516-1558) marks the fall of Catholic power through a sovereign totally devoted to that power and the consequent rise of individualism. In *The Foresters*, Tennyson took the twelfth century Earl of Huntingdon, already mythicized into a folk hero who stole from the rich to aid the poor, and accomplished his further transformation into a baron, siding with the disenfranchised poor against the depredations of both feudal aristocrats and tyrannical monarch, who together set the stage for the *Magna Carta* of 1215.

These four chronicle plays, more concerned with historical situations than individual characterization, do indeed constitute a magnificent proposal in an epical dramatic form. They exhibit wide diversities of treatment, style, and theme. *Harold* raises the entirely modern question— Is absolute personal integrity an option for a successful political leader? The drama is haunted by the active consequences of promises made, kept, or broken: Edward the Confessor's designation of Norman William as his heir; Harold's broken promise on the bones of Frankish saints and martyrs to support that designation (in order to release his hostage brother); Harold's kept promise to his father never voluntarily to turn England over to the Normans; Harold's broken promise to wed Edith (because Edward had destined her to a life of prayer as penance for the sins of his house); William's broken promise to release Harold's brother; the broken promise of the Danish-descended brethren of Aldwyth to support Harold; the many promises passionately made and lightly broken by and to hot-headed Tostig.

Harold is also haunted by a secular ruler, Edward the Confessor, who most desires a withdrawn life of monasticism, but instead is forced to unsuccessfully balance the claims of God and Mammon. This fits aptly with Tennyson's earlier contention that Ulysses, having been twenty years absent at the Trojan War, ought to stay home, comfort his "aging wife," and rule his contentious people. If anyone should have the prerogative of "always roaming with a hungry heart," it ought to be the young Telemachus rather than the elderly Ulysses. Likewise Arthur's knights, in his absence, committed themselves to the Quest for the Holy Grail. Their angry king berates them, calling most of them fit to break heads in the righting of civic wrongs, but callous and insensitive in the area of mystic vision. Arthus even claims to have visionary powers of his own, but muted and constrained by his duty to rule Camelot.

Becket, the drama least deplored by Tennyson critics, displayed the tight-drawn tension between a headstrong king and the loving but stubborn friend he elevated to Privy Seal and Archbishopric. Becket thus becomes a male version of Sophocles' Antigone. She mourned two brothers, Eteocles given a hero's entombment and Polynices left unburied. In the choice between obedience to her uncle-sovereign's edict and familial loyalty that enjoined her to sprinkle the earth and shed the wine that would permit Polynices to enter Hades, she chooses the religious over the civil. So Becket, filled with grateful love for the friend who had lifted him so high, could not finally sacrifice his personal honor or the Honor of God when his friend demanded the pay-back.

Queen Mary is a lengthy and powerful study of a woman who always meant the right that turned wrong. Loving the Catholic Church, she lost England for Catholicism. Promising that "no one in her time should be burnt for heresy," she is nicknamed "Bloody Mary" by history. Striving to make island England a part of the great European world order through her mother, Catherine of Aragon and her absentee husband Philip II of Spain, she forever turned the English against Spain and any fellowship with the worldwide Spanish Empire. Desiring always to be a good, modest wife and mother she put personal goals above national destiny and bore no children.

Just as Harold is haunted by the still powerful ghost of Edward the Confessor, turning the throne room into a priory and spending the throne's income on the dubious bones of puissant saints, so Mary is haunted by the failed marriages of Henry VIII, the disenfranchised Catherine of Aragon and the ascetic Holy Roman Emperor-in-retirement, Charles V. These withdrawn potentates join a major theme of Tennyson's poetry— those who, born to be kings, slipped back into a spiritual devotion which produced evasion of civic duty.

The Foresters is a charming drama of Sherwood Forest with the positive increment of a baron (Earl of Huntingdon-Robin Hood) instrumental in the brief jointure of aristocrat, yeoman, and peasant to trim aristocratic and monarchic authority, a document which we know as *Magna Carta*. On the negative side—since Tennyson was always engrossed in the balancing of antinomies—without exactly saying so, the play unmistakably suggests that the untrammeled Forest is an Eden of true love and neighborliness, whereas castle and town represent a fallen world, East of Eden, where only few of the ground rules of Utopia can be applied. The cheerful mood of the play is all the more poignant when we recall that the absent Richard Coeur de Lion, first on the Third Crusade, then as a hostage in Austria, then as the hostage of Holy Roman Emperor Henry VI, then returned to England to the stirring tones of Tennyson's chorus: "Now the King is home again, and nevermore to roam again," actually spent the total of only six months in England, using it merely as a milk-cow for his enormous ransom and as a base of operations for his European projects. So the old problem of an absentee from civic responsibility is not only raised yet once again, but becomes the central problem of a chronicle play.

In my examination of Tennyson's historical drama I found other plays of similar intent crowding in for attention. Thus *Becket* seemed somehow incomplete without comparison with T.S. Eliot's wryly-theological *Murder in the Cathedral* and Jean Anouilh's historically-inept *Becket ou L'Honneur de Dieu*. Tennyson's Becket is a man of flesh and blood instead of the bloodless cleric of Eliot; he is a man capable of lasting love by comparison with Henry II's darting, spasmodic passions; he is not like Anouilh's Becket, caught in the toils of a homosexual struggle with his male lover. The towering intellect of Eleanor of Aquitaine does not appear for Eliot. For Anouilh she is a flat-faced whiner parading her catalogue of marital woes. For Tennyson she is a great member of the troubadour tradition, a thinker able to assess the currents that flow about her inattentive husband, a wily plotter for the sons she can control against the husband she cannot.

Somehow it seemed difficult to discuss Mary Tudor and her longing for a husband and a child, without evoking comparison with Guinevere's disloyalty to her husband and childlessness, and Victoria of Saxe-Coburg, widow who could never forget her beloved Albert to whom she had borne nine heirs. Thus, by reference to the drama, to *Idylls of the King*, and the Anniversary poems to Queen-Empress, I made the combination chapter "Three Queens."

The Foresters, which found the source of evil in an absent ruler and the towns of power, immediately suggested William Wordsworth's *The Borderers*, likewise set in the outdoor world, but exploring the positive evil of a villain and the suggested evil of a man built for goodness.

When one concentrates upon Tennyson's epic drama (almost never done by literary critics) one tends to find drama in unexpected places. About the explosive dramatic zest of his juvenile (written at the age of fourteen) *The Devil and the Lady*, there can be no question of genre. It's the ramming of the barrel which waits fifty-three years to shoot its four cartridges. *The Princess*, a medley set in a Victorian frame, can more easily be read as a dramatic dialogue in seven scenes on the controversial issue of education for women rather than as a Beatrice/Benedick (*Much Ado About Nothing*) initial antagonism that finally surrenders into love. *Maud* Tennyson subtitled *A Monodrama*. Reading it aloud to Mr. J.T. Knowles, the Laureate described it as "a drama where successive stages of passion in one person take the place of successive persons." The Spasmodic passions of the hero clearly mark the work as most at home on the stage, rather than the rural countryside. Other critics, contemporaries of Tennyson and critics of our own age have seen the *Idylls of the King* as the three acts of a political tragedy in which the ideal king is finally ushered to the last great battle (Armageddon) before his wounding (Crucifixion), his translation (Apotheosis) to a far country whence he may one day return (Second Coming).

It seems significant that these works, not usually considered as dramas, are both more coherent and powerful when read as plays. The corollary is also true: if great standard works reveal aspects of drama—is the unmistakable drama not also a part of Tennyson's great standard works?

The Cup and *The Falcon* were extremely popular on British and American stages. The former, taken from Plutarch, the latter from Boccaccio, are short plays which should take their place among Tennyson's Classical work ("Ulysses," "Tithonus," and "Oenone") and his medieval/renaissance poems (*Idylls of the King*, "The Lover's Tale"). So brief they were either combined or presented along with a popular curtain-raiser to make a full Victorian evening at the theatre. *The Falcon* is highly-contrived and built upon a *climax fausse* with formerly estranged hero and heroine echoing "I am happy." Short but elaborate in tone and diction, it was sure-fire dramatic fare. *The Cup* wears its laurels for quite different characteristics. The tone and diction practice Classical restraint, but the action presents the savage revenge of a heroic widow taken upon her husband's murderer. With no particular male heroes, the play has heroism enough in the stunning self-immolation of the tragic heroine.

A domestic idyll turned tragic, like *Maud*, *The Promise of May* is unique for two reasons. First, the Poet Laureate is writing drama in deliberately bucolic prose. Second, the drama sets itself to examine, from philosophic and psychological scrutiny, the diagnosis of the English "wrongs against youth" as originally presented in the ringing fustian poetry of "Locksley Hall" and "Locksley Hall Sixty Years After." The Old England, prose with a rural accent, sets itself against a villain with collegiate accent poisoned by the unbelief of the age. Accepting the challenge to be contemporary issued by Carlyle and Ruskin, Tennyson depicts two worlds in collision, one old, agrarian, and faithful,—the other new, modern, careless and callous. In the collision it would seem that both worlds are annihilated. Farmer Dobson can never win a philosophic argument against Squire Edgar. But Edgar is crushed beneath implacable biology and an old-fashioned virtue which refuses to die. So the confrontation is inevitably tragic and Tennyson moves with its irresistible logic.

For critics who tend to see Tennyson only as "the mourning muse," the singer of sad songs, the Laureate's leap from the Jacobean fragment *The Devil and the Lady* to seven dramas in eight years did find dramatic paving stones along the way. Real dramatic passions throb through "The Two Voices," "The Palace of Art," "The Lotos-Eaters," "Tithonus," the two "Locksley Halls," *Maud, Idylls of the King,* "Demeter and Persephone," *In Memoriam.* Real national fervor sings its way into popular song in his "Ode on the Duke of Wellington," "The Charge of the Light Brigade," "Boadicea," "The Defense of Lucknow," "The Charge of the Heavy Brigade," "Hands All Round." Real identification with rural England thickens its accents in the now-unpopular "The Miller's Daughter," *Enoch Arden*, "Northern Farmer: Old Style, New Style," "The Northern Cobbler," "The Village Wife."

The extraordinary outpouring of drama between 1875-1882 not only revealed salient points in the personality of England, it also expanded themes earlier treated in brief poems and summarized what the grateful, but critical, Poet Laureate had to say to his country about its past, its present, and its veiled future.

Bibliography

BOOKS

Baum, Paull F. *Tennyson Sixty Years After*. Chapel Hill: University of North Carolina Press, 1948.

Brooke, Stopford A. *Tennyson: His Art and Relation to Modern Life*. London and New York: G. P. Putnam's Sons, 1899.

Brooks, Cleanth. *Modern Poetry and the Tradition*. Chapel Hill: University of North Carolina Press, 1939.

Buckley, Jerome Hamilton. *The Victorian Temper: A Study in Literary Culture*. Cambridge, Massachusetts: Harvard University Press, 1951.

Bush, Douglas. *Mythology and the Romantic Tradition*. Cambridge, Massachusetts: Harvard University Press, 1937.

Cruse, Amy. *The Victorians and Their Reading*. Boston: Houghton Mifflin, 1935.

Eggers, J. Philip. *King Arthur's Laureate: A Study of Tennyson's "Idylls of the King."* New York: New York University Press, 1971.

Foucault, Michel. *Madness and Civilization: A History of Insanity in the Age of Reason*. Trans. Richard Howard. New York: Vintage Books, 1965.

Goslee, David. *Tennyson's Characters: "Strange Faces, Other Minds."* Iowa City: University of Iowa Press, 1989.

Hair, Donald J. *Domestic and Heroic in Tennyson's Poetry*. Toronto, Canada: Toronto University Press, 1981.

Henderson, Philip. *Tennyson, Poet and Prophet*. London: Routledge & Kegan Paul, 1978.

Huckel, Oliver. *Through England with Tennyson: A Pilgrimage to Places Associated with the Great Laureate*. Chatauqua, New York: Chatauqua Press, 1913.

Hughes, Linda K. *The Manyfacèd Glass: Tennyson's Dramatic Monologues*. Athens, Ohio. London: Ohio University Press, 1987.

Irving, Lawrence. *Henry Irving: The Actor and His World*. London: Faber & Faber, 1951.

Japikse, Cornelia G. *Dramas of Alfred, Lord Tennyson*. No. 27: Studies in Tennyson, 1969.

Johnson, Wendell Stacy. *Sex and Marriage in Victorian Poetry*. Ithaca: Cornell University Press, 1975.

Jones, Richard. *The Growth of the "Idylls of the King."* Philadelphia: J.B. Lippincott, 1895.

Joseph, Gerhard. *Tennysonian Love: The Strange Diagonal*. Minneapolis: University of Minnesota Press, 1969.

———. *Tennyson and the Text: The Weaver's Shuttle.* Cambridge University Press, 1992.

Killham, John. *Tennyson and The Princess: Reflections of an Age.* London: Athlone Press, 1958.

Langbaum, Robert. *The Poetry of Experience: The Dramatic Monologue in Modern Literary Tradition.* London: Chatto & Windus, 1957.

Levi, Peter. *Tennyson.* New York: Charles Scribner's Sons, 1993.

Lucas, Frank Laurence. *Ten Victorian Poets.* New York: Macmillan, 1948.

———. *Tennyson.* London, New York, Toronto: Longmans, Green, 1957.

Lytton, Edward Bulwer. *Harold, The Last of the Saxon Kings*, 2 vols. New York: Charles Scribner's Sons, 1903.

MacCallum, M.W. *Tennyson's "Idylls of the King" an Arthurian Story from the Sixteenth Century.* Glasgow: MacLehose, 1894.

Malory, Sir Thomas. *Morte d'Arthur.* Thomas Wright, ed. London: Reeves and Turner, 1889.

Martin, Robert Bernard. *Tennyson: The Unquiet Heart.* New York: Oxford University Press, 1980.

McGann, Jerome J. *The Beauty of Inflections: Literary Investigations in Historical Method and Theory.* Oxford University Press, 1985.

Miller, J. Hillis. *The Disappearance of God.* Cambridge: Harvard University Press, 1963.

Organ, Dennis M. *Tennyson's Dramas: A Critical Study.* Graduate Studies, Texas Technical University, no. 17. Lubbock: Texas Technical Press, 1970.

Ormond, Leonée. *History and Drama,* "Alfred Tennyson: A Literary Life." New York: St. Martin's Press, 1993.

Otten, T.J. *Tennyson's "Maud" and "Becket," The Deserted Stage: The Search for Dramatic Form in Nineteenth Century England.* Athens, Ohio: Ohio University Press, 1972.

Pattison, Robert. *Tennyson and Tradition.* Cambridge: Harvard University Press, 1979.

Peltason, Timothy. *Reading "In Memoriam."* Princeton University Press, 1985.

Platizky, Roger S. *A Blueprint of His Dissent: Madness and Method in Tennyson's Poetry.* Lewisburg: Bucknell University Press, London and Toronto; Associated University Presses, 1989.

Priestley, F.E.L. *Language and Structure in Tennyson's Poetry.* London: Andre Deutsch, 1973.

Reed, John R. *Perception and Design in Tennyson's "Idylls of the King."* Athens: Ohio University Press, 1969.

Richardson, Joanna. "Laureate and Lyceum" and "Plays and Tragedies," *The Pre-Eminent Victorian: A Study of Tennyson.* Westport, Connecticut: Greenwood Press, 1962.

Ricks, Christopher. *Tennyson.* New York: The Macmillan Company, 1972.
———. and Aidan Day, eds. *The Tennyson Archive.* 30 vols. New York.
Rolfe, W.J., ed. *The Complete Poetical Works of Tennyson.* Boston: Houghton Mifflin Company, 1898.
Rosenberg, John D. *The Fall of Camelot: A Study of Tennyson's "Idylls of the King."* Cambridge: Harvard University Press, 1973.
Ryals, Clyde de L. *From the Great Deep: Essays on "Idylls of the King."* Athens, Ohio: Ohio University Press, 1967.
Sharma, Virendra. *Studies in Victorian Verse Drama.* Salzburg Studies in English Literature, no. 14. Salzburg: Institut für Anglistik und Amerikanistik, Universität Salzburg, 1979.
Shaw, W. David. *Tennyson's Style.* Ithaca: Cornell University Press, 1976.
Sinfield, Alan. *Dramatic Monologue.* Critical Idiom Series, no. 36. Methuen & Company, 1977.
Smith, Elton Edward. *The Two Voices: A Tennyson Study.* Lincoln: University of Nebraska Press, 1964.
Tennyson, Charles. *Alfred Tennyson.* New York: Macmillan Company, 1949.
Tennyson, Hallam. *Alfred, Lord Tennyson: A Memoir by His Son.* 2 vols. London: Macmillan Company, 1898.
Terhune, A. McKinley. *Life of Edward FitzGerald.* New Haven: Yale University Press, 1947.
Thorn, Michael. *Tennyson.* New York: St. Martin's Press, 1992.
Tucker, Herbert F. *Tennyson and the Doom of Romanticism.* Cambridge, Massachusetts: Harvard University Press, 1988.
Waugh, Arthur. *Alfred, Lord Tennyson: A Study of the Life and Works.* London: Heinemann, 1892.
Weigert, Edith. *The Courage to Love.* New Haven: Yale University

ESSAYS

Archer, William. *English Dramatics of Today.* London: Sampson Low, Marston, Searle, & Rivington, 1882.
Bagehot, Walter. "Wordsworth, Tennyson and Browning" (1864), in *English Critical Essays: Nineteenth Century,* ed. Edmund D. Jones. Oxford: Oxford University Press, 1945.
Byatt, A.S. "The Lyric Structure of Tennyson's 'Maud,'" in *Major Victorian Poets: Reconsiderations,* ed. Isobel Armstrong. Lincoln: University of Nebraska Press, 1969.
Devlin, Francis. "Dramatic Irony in the Early Sections of Tennyson's 'In Memoriam'" *Papers on Language and Literature* 8, 1972.
Francis, Elizabeth, ed. *Tennyson: A Collection of Critical Essays.* Englewood Cliffs, N.J.: Prentice Hall, 1980.

Fredeman, William E. "One Word More — on Tennyson's Dramatic Monologues." *Studies in Tennyson*, ed. Hallam Tennyson. Totowa, N.J.: Barnes & Noble, 1981.

Granville-Barker, Harley, ed. "Tennyson, Swinburne, Meredith — and the Theatre." *The Eighteen-Seventies: Essays by Fellows of the Royal Society of Literature*. Cambridge: Cambridge University Press, 1929.

Killham, John, ed. *Critical Essays on the Poetry of Tennyson*. New York: Barnes & Noble, 1960. Relevant Contents:
 E. J. Chiasson, "Tennyson's 'Ulysses' — a Re-Interpretation"
 H. M. McLuhan, "Tennyson and the Romantic Epic"
 F. E. D. Priestley, "Tennyson's Idylls"
 W. W. Robson, "The Dilemma of Tennyson"

Knight, G. Wilson. "Victorian," *The Golden Labyrinth: A Study of British Drama*. London: Phoenix House, 1962.

Larkin, Philip. "The Most Victorian Laureate," *Required Writing: Miscellaneous Pieces 1955-1982*. New York: Farrar, Straus, & Giroux, 1982.

Lucas, Frank Laurence. *Ten Victorian Poets*. New York: Macmillan, 1948.

Page, Norman. "Larger Hopes and the New Hedonism," in Philip Collins, ed. *Tennyson: Seven Essays*. Houndmills: The Macmillan Press Ltd., 1992.

Simpson, Roger. *Camelot Regained: The Arthurian Revival and Tennyson 1800-1849*. Arthurian Studies XXI, D.S. Brewer.

Thomson, Peter. "Tennyson's Plays and Their Production," in D. J. Palmer, ed. *Tennyson*. Writers and Their Background Series. London: George Bell and Sons, 1973.

PERIODICAL ARTICLES

Basler, Roy. "Tennyson the Psychologist." *South Atlantic Quarterly* 43 (1944), 143-159.

Bennett, James R. "The Historical Abuse of Literature: Tennyson's 'Maud: A Monodrama' and the Crimean War." *English Studies* 62 (1981), 34-35.

Boyd, Zelda, and Julian Boyd. "To Lose the Name of Action: The Semantics of Action and Motion in Tennyson's Poetry." *PTL: A Journal for Descriptive Poetics and Theory* 2 (1977), 21-32.

Cadbury, William. "Tennyson's 'The Palace of Art' and the Rhetoric of Structures." *Criticism* 7 (1965), 23-44.

Culler, A. Dwight. "Monodrama and the Dramatic Monologue." *PMLA* 90 (1975), 366-385.

Devlin, Francis. "Dramatic Irony in the Early Sections of Tennyson's *In Memoriam*," *Papers on Language and Literature* 8 (1972), 172-183.

Draper, Anita B. "The Artistic Contribution of the 'Weird Seizures' to *The Princess." Victorian Poetry* 17 (1979), 180-191.

Eidson, John Olin. "The Reception of Tennyson's Plays in America," *Philological Quarterly* 35 (1956), 435-443.

Fredeman, William E. "'The Sphere of Common Duties:' The Domestic Solution in Tennyson's Poetry." *Bulletin of the John Rylands Library* 54 (1972), 357-383.

Giordano, Frank, Jr. "'The Red-Ribbed Hollow,' Suicide and Part III of *Maud." Notes & Queries* 24 (1977), 402-404.

Grosskurth, Phyllis. "Tennyson, Froude, and *Queen Mary." Tennyson Research Bulletin* (1973), 44-54.

Hobsbaum, Philip. "The Rise of the Dramatic Monologue." *Hudson Review* 28 (1975), 227-245.

James, Henry. "Tennyson's Drama." *Views & Reviews.* Boston, Massachusetts: The Ball Publishing Company, 1908.

Johnson, E.D.H. "The Lily and the Rose: Symbolic Meaning in Tennyson's *Maud.*" PMLA 64 (1949), 1222-1227.

Johnson, W. Stacy. "The Theme of Marriage in Tennyson." *Victorian Newsletter*, XII (Fall 1957), 8-14.

Killham, John. "Tennyson and the Sinful Queen—A Corrected Impression." *Notes and Queries* n.s. 5(1958), 507-511.

Korg, Jacob. "The Pattern of Fatality in Tennyson's Poetry." *Victorian Newsletter*, XIV (Fall 1958), 8-11.

O'Donnell, Angela G. "Tennyson's English Idylls: Studies in Poetic Decorum." Studies in *Philology*, LXXXV, no. 1 (Winter 1988), 125-144.

Rader, Ralph. "The Dramatic Monologue and Related Lyric Forms." *Critical Inquiry* 3 (1976), 131-151.

Rehak, Louise Rouse. "On the Use of Martyrs: Tennyson and Eliot on Thomas Becket." *University of Toronto Quarterly* 33 (1963-1964), 44-60.

Rosenbaum, Jean Watson. "Apples and Milkmaids: The Visionary Experience in Tennyson's The Holy Grail." *Studia Mystica* 4 (1981), 11-35.

Salt, James E. "Tennyson's *The Princess* and *Queen Mary*: Two Examinations of Sex and Politics." *Durham University Journal* 37 (1975), 70-78.

Solimene, Joseph. "The Dialectics of Church and State: Tennyson's Historical Plays." *The Personalist* XLVII (1966), 218-225.

Tucker, Herbert F., Jr. "From Monomania to Monologue: St. Simeon Stylites and the Rise of the Victorian Dramatic Monologue." *Victorian Poetry* 22 (1984), 121-137.

Weissman, Judith. "Vision, Madness and Morality: Poetry and the Theory of the Bicameral Mind." *Georgia Review* 33 (1979), 118-148.

Wimsatt, W.K., Jr. "*Prufrock* and *Maud*: From Plot to Symbol." *Yale French Studies* 9 (1952), 84-92.

LETTERS

Kolb, Jack, ed. *The Letters of Arthur Henry Hallam*. Columbus: Ohio State University Press, 1981.

Lang, Cecil Y. and Edgar F. Shannon, Jr., eds. *The Letters of Alfred Lord Tennyson*, vol. III 1871-1892. Clarendon Press, Oxford: 1990.

Alfred McKinley Terhune and Annabelle Berdick Terhune, eds. *The Letters of Edward FitzGerald*. Princeton University Press, 1980.

PLAYS

1823-1824 *The Devil and the Lady* (uncompleted play from Juvenilia, unpublished during the playwright's lifetime)

1875 *Queen Mary* (produced 1876)

1876-1877 *Harold* (not produced in the 19th century)

1882 *The Promise of May* (only prose drama; produced 1882)

1884 *The Cup* (produced in 1881)

The Falcon (produced in 1879)

Becket (produced in 1899)

1892 *The Foresters* (produced in 1892)

The plays are included in the 85th volume, Eversley Edition, *The Works of Lord Tennyson, Annotated*, and in the 89th volume of the *Oxford Standard Authors*.

Anouilh, Jean. *Becket ou l'Honneur de Dieu*. La Table Ronde 40, rue de Bac-VIIe, Paris, 1959.

Eliot, T.S. *Murder in the Cathedral*. New York: Harcourt, Brace and Company, 1935.

Wordsworth, William. *The Borderers, The Poetical Works of William Wordsworth*, William Knight, ed. vol. I. Edinburgh: William Paterson, 1882.

Tennyson, Charles, ed. *The Devil and the Lady*. Bloomington: Indiana University Press, 1964.

Tennyson, Hallam, Lord, ed. *Becket and Other Plays*. London: Macmillan Company, Ltd., 1908.

Warren, T, Herbert, ed. *The Complete Poetical Works of Tennyson*. London: Oxford University Press, 1953.

BIBLIOGRAPHIES

Major collections of the Tennyson manuscripts may be found at Trinity College, Cambridge; Houghton Library, Harvard University; Berg Collection, New York Public Library; Huntington Library; British Museum; Tennyson Research Centre, Lincoln.

Collins, Rowland. "The Frederick Tennyson Collection," *Victorian Studies* VII (Christmas Supplement 1963), 56-76.

Ricks, Christopher. "The Tennyson Manuscripts at Trinity College, Cambridge," *Times Literary Supplement* (21 August 1969) 918-922.

———. "Spedding's Annotations of the Trinity MS of *In Memoriam*," *Tennyson Research Bulletin* (1984) 110-113.

Ricks, Christopher and Day, Aidan, eds. *The Tennyson Archive*, 30 vols. New York: Garland Publishing.

Shannon, Edgar F. and Bond, W.H. "Literary Manuscripts of Alfred Tennyson in the Harvard College Library," *Harvard Library Bulletin*. X (1956), 254-274.

Shaw, Marion. A*n Annotated Critical Bibliography of Alfred, Lord Tennyson*. Hempstead: Harvester Wheatsheaf, St. Martin's Press, 1989.

Tennyson, Charles. "Tennyson Papers II. J.M. Heath's 'Commonplace Book,'" *Cornhill Magazine* CLIII (April 1936), 426-496.

Index